AIRLINE CAE
Interview and Ca

GW01072169

First Editio

Copyright © 2022 Margɩ   ...ɩ0w

All rights reserved.

ISBN: 978-1-9163361-1-7

Printed in the United Kingdom

10 9 8 7 6 5 4 3 2 1

Library of Congress Cataloging-in-Publication Data
A CIP catalogue record for this book can be obtained from the
British Library

Contents

Disclaimer

This book is designed to provide information and guidance on attending a cabin crew assessment. It is sold with the understanding that the publisher and author are not engaged in rendering legal or other professional services. Such topics, as discussed herein are, for example, or illustrative purposes only. If expert assistance is required, the services of a competent professional should be sought where you can explore the unique aspects of your situation.

It is not the purpose of this guide to reprint all the information that is otherwise available to candidates but instead to complement, amplify and supplement other texts. You are urged to read all the available material, learn as much as possible about the role and interview techniques and tailor the information to your individual needs.

Every effort has been made to make this guide as complete and accurate as possible. However, this guide contains information that is current only up to the printing date. Interview processes are frequently updated and are often subject to differing interpretations. Therefore, there are no absolutes and this text should be used only as a general guide and not as the ultimate source of information.

All information in this book is offered as an opinion of the author and should be taken as such and used with discretion by the reader. You are solely responsible for your use of this book. Neither the publisher nor the author explicitly or implicitly promises that readers will find employment because of anything written or implied here.

The author shall have neither liability nor responsibility to you or anyone else because of any information contained in or left out of this book.

The views and opinions expressed within this guide are those of the author and do not represent the views of any airlines or organisations named within. Any airlines mentioned are for the purpose of demonstration only. This book is neither associated, approved, affiliated with, nor endorsed by any airline.

Course Overview

The cabin crew interview proficiency program provides comprehensive instruction on navigating an airlines' cabin crew selection process.

Throughout, you will learn pragmatic, tried and tested, and immediately applicable information which helps you successfully navigate this tricky-though-logical, multi-stage selection process.

It is designed to take you from theory to application, forming knowledge and skills that move you towards your goal of becoming a member of airline cabin crew.

Course Objectives

Our objective is to facilitate your successful employment as cabin crew with the airline of your choice. To achieve this objective, we provide you with usable and practical solutions, in a step-by-step format that you can implement today with complete confidence.

Level of Study

This course is suitable for all levels, whether you are new to airline recruitment processes, are a seasoned applicant, or even if you have relative industry experience.

Depending on your level of experience and desired areas of focus, you will be able to customize your learning with various routes we have mapped out for you.

Pre-Requisites

In order to qualify for a position of cabin crew, you will need to meet certain minimum requirements.

The following guidelines will give you a clear lay of the land so you know what to expect throughout the course and help you prepare for a pleasant journey through the curriculum.

We hope that you find this course informing and fun.

Career Outlook

While no two airlines are the same, and there are some variances in hiring processes, the information packed into this course is universal and transferrable, revealing how airlines screen and hire all across the world, from the largest international carriers to the smallest national operators.

To supplement the foundation materials, we have included several specialised airline guides for some of the most popular airlines. Within these guides, you will find done-for-you cheatsheets, complete breakdowns of the hiring process and useful resources to aide you in your journey.

Graduates of this course have gone on to work for top airlines, such as Emirates, Virgin Atlantic, British Airways, and American Airlines, to name but a few. Of course we will be encouraging you to pursue your dream airline too.

General Outline

The course is made up of four foundational phases, each containing multiple sections and modules. Here is a high level overview of the course structure:

- The initiation phase
- The discovery phase
- The preparation phase
- The practical phase

This organised sequence of theoretical and practical lessons build on basic skills to achieve a higher level of airline interview proficiency.

You'll be taken behind the scenes to discover the ins and outs of airline hiring processes from the recruiters point of view. This knowledge will empower you to enter the process with a sense of ease and increased confidence.

It is designed to take you from theory to application, forming knowledge and skills that move you towards your goal of becoming a member of airline cabin crew.

Materials Included

To cater to a diverse range of learning styles and assist in your overall development and comprehension, you will have access to several formats of learning materials, these include:

- Handbooks
- Workbooks
- Logbooks
- Video presentations
- Audio tutorials
- Crew portal

- Crew App

Complimentary entertainment, practical worksheets and interactive learning exercises are provided on board each route. These materials are an extension of your foundational materials and are valuable resources that will help facilitate your comprehension and retention. These are optional, but highly recommended for an enhanced learning experience.

To fine tune your knowledge and expertise, there are suggested review sessions associated with each stage of your journey. You do not have to complete them, however, we strongly advise that you do. These are designed to:

- Supplement the theory and instruction, and
- enhance learning by identifying weak areas

Course Delivery

Online education is the ideal way to prepare for your cabin crew career whilst still comfortably honouring other work or family commitments. For this reason, all interactive course content can be accessed via our Virtual Learning Platform (VLP) via the internet using your computer.

Because the resources are digital, they are immediately available to study anywhere that is convenient for you, and are always up to date.

For your convenience, materials will be available for download in easy to read pdf and ePub formats that you can access on various reading devices.

Course Schedule

This course is self-paced, independent study, in an online environment.

From start to finish, this course will take approximately 46 hours to complete. This includes your reading, and module activities.

The course is most effective if the itinerary is completed in sequence, particularly if you are new to cabin crew selection processes. Having said that, this course is designed to be a self-paced, independent study. Therefore, depending on your level of experience and time allocation you will be able to fully customize your learning with the various routes we have mapped out for you.

While you are responsible for scheduling your study time, below is a list of guidelines for effective online studying and progression:

- Go through the various routes in Departures to find the best approach for you
- Establish a schedule and set clear expectations for your training
- Schedule study time for the material daily
- Complete your assignments and quizzes at the end of each section
- Participate actively in the Portal

Progressing Through the Syllabus

The course is most effective if the training is completed in sequence, particularly if you are new to cabin crew selection processes. Having said that, you can work ahead as far as you like at your own discretion.

There are two routes included and these are designed to allow for flexibility in obtaining the level of proficiency you wish to achieve and the time you have available. These routes include:

- Direct (Short and concise)

- Connecting (Detailed)

Direct is an expedited route designed to give more flexibility to your needs. This route is ideal for those who are :

- Working under tight time constraints
- Former cabin crew
- Alumni

The connecting route contains detailed content. It is designed for candidates who want to prepare thoroughly. This route is ideal for those who are seeking a complete step by step blueprint to follow.

Integrating Outside Learning

Independent study is a key part of the course. Links to useful resources are given throughout and directly respond to a module's content. It is recommended that you use all available resources, including those above and beyond what is listed for the route plan.

Scenario Based Training

Reality is the ultimate learning situation, and scenario-based training attempts to get as close as possible to this ideal. The more realistic the training scenario, the better you learn core safety habits and decision-making skills that can be applied in the real-world.

Scenario-Based Training (SBT) uses real-world scenarios as the foundation of training. The use of real-world scenarios presents situations and circumstances that cabin crew face every day as learning experiences.

For the purposes of this course, we have developed a Scenario-Based Training program specifically for the cabin crew selection process.

These learning experiences fall into five scenarios.

- Skill-Based Scenario — the learner is expected to demonstrate skills and knowledge they have already acquired; it works best after a theoretical session or at least a short workshop in which some basic information is covered (or merely dusted off);
- Problem-Based Scenario — this is ideal for stances in which learners need to tap both into their theoretical and practical knowledge to figure out the ramifications of a problem. Decision-making, logical reasoning, and critical thinking are all necessary in dealing with this type of scenario;

- Issue-Based Scenario — not necessarily looking for a clear-cut resolution, learners are asked to take a stand on issues, usually with humanitarian perspectives, and think about these in order to understand the bigger picture;
- Speculative Scenario — learners are asked to predict the outcome of an event in the future based on what they know at the present time and how they feel things are evolving (they have to tap into their own intuition);
- Gaming Scenario — probably the most fun kind, these scenarios involve the use of games as learning tools.

To achieve this objective we provide you with usable and practical solutions, in a variety of formats, that you can implement today with complete confidence.

This organised sequence of theoretical and practical lessons build on basic skills to achieve a higher level of airline interview proficiency.

You'll be taken behind the scenes to discover the ins and outs of airline hiring processes from the recruiters point of view. This knowledge will empower you to enter the process with a sense of ease and increased confidence.

Reality is the ultimate learning situation, and scenario-based training attempts to get as close as possible to this ideal. The more realistic the training scenario

- The better you learn core safety habits, and
- Decision-making skills that can be applied in the real-world.

Scenario-Based Training (SBT) uses real-world scenarios as the foundation of training. The use of real-world scenarios presents situations and circumstances that cabin crew face every day as learning experiences.

Undercover Operations

The undercover recruiter

It is by no means a secret that candidates rarely show their true selves during a formal interview process. They will do their best to say all the right things, hide undesirable traits and say what they think the recruiters want to hear. After all, it is only natural that you'll want to be seen in the best possible light. The problem is, this makes it extremely difficult for personnel to accurately gage whether any one particular candidate is truly a good fit for the job, the airline and its corporate culture, or is just playing a very good part for the interview.

The task of filtering through hundreds or thousands of applicants is an arduous one and, to make matters worse, there are only a few short hours in which to accomplish it.

To relieve some of this pressure, undercover personnel are often placed among the group during recruitment days. It is these undercover officers who pose the greatest threat to your ultimate success, as their primary objective is to filter and eliminate candidates as quickly as possible, and for any reason they see fit. They are largely accountable for the high percentage of failure rates and are the reason why many candidates leave the interview feeling confused about their elimination.

Hidden assessments

From the moment you step foot on the airline's territory, these officers are watching and judging your every move.

Your personal conduct, how you interact socially and professionally, and the information you reveal. are constantly being scrutinised and assessed. Any mishap or red flags raised during this crucial encounter can land your resume in the rejection pile and you to the nearest exit. There are no second chances.

Within the guise of a fellow candidate, these officers can observe individuals in their relaxed and natural state, and be in a better position to extract information. Unsuspecting candidates openly volunteer information that would never otherwise be revealed, as they are lulled into a false sense of security with seemingly harmless dialogue only to be enticed into mindless gossip and other undesirable behaviours.

During this critical period, officers are observing the reactions of candidates closely as they are encouraged to reciprocate and reveal all sorts of personal and private information. The observations made are then periodically fed back to the recruitment team, who are able to use the information to make informed decisions and better elimination choices in record speed.

It's not what you think

These officers are not interested in your level of education, previous successes, or best attributes; they are there to uncover information that could potentially cause problems or inconvenience for the airline. As such, the information gathered at this level is not necessarily sized up against the airline's corporate culture and assessment criteria, but rather the hidden criterion and person specification.

It is the information candidates reveal about their health, age, their likes and dislikes, and sensitive information about their background and personal life that are of interest to these officers. Likewise, they will be very interested to learn how you react to certain kinds of behaviours, people and pressures.

Needless to say, a candidate who displays undesirable behaviour or reveal questionable information will not proceed very far.

Shocking revelations

It never seizes to amaze me how much information unsuspecting candidates will reveal when they think they are not being assessed. In many instances, it isn't even necessary to cajole candidates into confessing information, as many will openly share all sorts of things. Is it really any wonder airlines use undercover personnel?

Here are just some of the revelations I have encountered during my on site excursions.

Under the influence

"I'm so nervous I think I must have drunk a whole bottle of wine before I arrived."

Bunking off work

"I had to take a sickie at work just to attend this interview, so it better be worth it."

Admissions of deceit

"I had to lie on my application just to get invited to this interview"

Malicious backbiting

"Did you see what that girl is wearing? What was she thinking?"

"That girl obviously has no brains. I bet she can't even read."

Negative intentions

"This is such a joke, I wanted to work for . . . but keep failing the damn interview so I have no choice but to apply for this one."

"I just want to work my way into first class so I can meet a rich, good looking guy"

The hangover

"I'm so hung over from last nights bash, I just want to go to sleep. Wake me when it's over."

Slandering the boss

"My stupid boss fired me, so I need this job desperately"

Many of these cases are rather extreme, I admit, however, they are by no means rare - I'm sure you've heard similar comments yourself.

As anyone can appreciate, it is these very mindless and irresponsible comments that undercover officers are seeking.

Innocent casualties

Unfortunately, candidates don't need to be malicious or brash to be excluded from the process. A candidate who innocently mentions their looming personal challenges, such as going through a separation, in a custody battle, recently been made redundant, experiencing financial difficulties, or dealing with a close family member who is in poor health, could raise red flags as to their focus and stability. While such challenges are common and entirely understandable, such circumstances are simply deemed too risky for an airline.

What to expect?

While the above shock statements were made by actual candidates, is it possible that such revelations could also be made by the undercover officers themselves as part of their mini assessment? Absolutely. It is precisely this kind of revelation that officers will use to entice a reaction or a reciprocal response. Be mindful, however, because such assessments aren't always this obvious or extreme.

Assessments can be covert and very sneaky, so you always need to be on your guard.

Just as new cabin crew hires are put through an intensive training program, so too are undercover officers. These officers are trained in behavioural analysis and psychological profiling and, with this training, they are able to take on a variety of different roles and employ many different tactics. This makes them very effective at blending in and there is little chance that you will ever be able to identify them with any certainty.

The good news is that simply being aware of their presence and being prepared with a strategy will give you an advantage like no other. In fact, your informed knowledge and inability to be culled by their tricks and traps will make you stand out as a top candidate among the crowd.

Even better still, there is much more that you can do, not only to evade their traps, but also turn them into your greatest ally. All that is required is a conscientious and diligent approach.

Your greatest ally

While it is accurate to say that the purpose of these undercover officers is to expose unsuitable candidates, they also have the power to approve candidates they deem to be exceptional.

If you are able to evade the tricks and traps laid out during this critical process and maintain a friendly, confident, and positive dialogue there will be no reason to pursue you further with trick questions. They will simply move on to another candidate when they are able to remove themselves from your presence. And if you are able to go one step further and create a connection with the officer, not only will you be put forward as a recommendation, but they will actually try to help you to succeed.

So how do you go about impressing these officers?

Create the right impression

To impress undercover officers, you simply need to treat everyone you meet in the same positive manner. If you are friendly, respectful and supportive towards your fellow candidates, have a positive outlook and are able to demonstrate an enthusiastic attitude towards any activities that you are asked to undertake, the officers will naturally pick up on your positive energy.

Moreover, it is important to remember that anything you say, even in jest or small talk, can and will be used against you. Thus you should avoid volunteering inappropriate information, and your personal life should remain personal.

Naturally this can be easier said than done, so I have devised a line-up of potential scenarios to help you recognise and diffuse any situation you may encounter.

The Lineup

Undercover officers are like actors. They come in many shapes and sizes and their pseudo personalities are just as diverse. Because you'll never really know whether a candidate is truly a candidate or an undercover officer, it is important that you treat everyone the same. Here is the line-up of the common personalities that you may come across and how to deal with each of them in an appropriate manner.

The show-off

You can be certain to find a show-off at every cabin crew interview. You will recognise him or her by their showy, self-absorbed and obnoxious attitude. While this personality type is easily annoying, the truth is that these individuals tend to be deeply insecure. They brag about their own achievements through fear that nobody will otherwise notice. Be kind and sincerely acknowledge their efforts when appropriate. This will demonstrate that you are not easily antagonised, but are also sensitive to the feelings of others.

The rival

In playing the part of the rival, the officer will demonstrate a very competitive streak, which puts you and everyone else as their competition and a threat to their success. They will attempt to make you feel inferior in order to throw you of guard. With these personality types, it is important to be friendly, but respectful of their space. Remember, competitive people are passionate, driven and innovative, so embrace these positive traits and don't let their feeling of superiority run you down.

The gossipmonger

Gossipmongers like to point out other people's flaws or failures in an attempt to feel superior. This personality type is a favourite amongst officers because it can reveal a great deal about a candidate. Are you passive or assertive? Do you engage in gossip or show disapproval?

The best defence in this scenario is to first neutralise the negative comment by pointing out a positive and contrary opinion and then attempting to change the subject. If you have a tenacious officer, they may continue to press. In this instance, it would be wise to respectfully state that you would rather not discuss the merits of others, as it is not your place to do so. This honest approach should dissolve any further discussion on the subject. Failing that, it would be best to take your leave immediately.

The think-they-know-it-all

Know-it-all's have an attitude of superiority and like to think they are experts in everything. In conversation, they are arrogant and condescending and openly disregard the opinion of others. Remain cordial and patient and, whatever you do, don't be drawn into a debate, become critical or impatient. If the so called expert becomes overbearing or it is obvious that they are not an expert at all, you assertiveness skill s may be being tested, so you may tactfully and respectfully state the facts as you perceive them.

The overly anxious

The part of an anxious candidate is a prime opportunity to observe your patience and sensitivity. Experiencing a heightened level of anxiety is very traumatic and paralysing, so be friendly and supportive with these individuals. Offer words of encouragement, but don't place too much focus on their anxiety. Rather, try to break their state by asking questions about things they enjoy and that make them feel relaxed. You could ask them about their hobbies or desires.

The negativist

Ah, the negativist. There's always one in every crowd and officers love to use this one to gauge a candidate's ability to remain positive under pressure. At best, negativists are very annoying. At worst, they will drain every ounce of energy and motivation from your body. If your attempts to motivate or encourage these people fall flat, remain positive and try to distance yourself as much as possible. If this is not possible, detach yourself from their words and stay focused on your own positive energy.

The aggressor

Passive aggressors are covert and manipulative. They disguise their attacks as constructive criticism or harmless jokes so that, in the instance that they are confronted, they can deny any wrong doing. If you find yourself under attack from these predators, you may ask questions that will temp them into the open, such as: "Forgive me, but that sounded like a disrespectful comment, was it?" In the worst case, you may try to distance yourself.

If the aggressor is more openly disrespectful and disparaging, the best approach is to remain calm and composed, listen attentively and without interruption until they have finished. A counter attack will only reflect badly on you, so resist the tendency to fight back. Instead, acknowledge their opinion and then voice your own in a respectful manner or simply remove yourself from them as much as possible.

The open book

If an individual airs all their dirty laundry to you, revealing all sorts of personal hardships, it could be that they are looking for a reciprocal response. You may demonstrate empathy for their situation, but avoid getting drawn too deeply into conversation about of their hardship and avoid revealing any of your own. Changing the subject and pointing out the positive is always the best course of action.

The usual suspects

The aforementioned scenarios are rather obvious, so they are generally easier to contend with. Where the traps really lie are in those personalities, which are not negative at all. In fact, it is the positive personalities, such as those in the following scenarios, which will often catch a candidate off guard. Because these personality types are friendly, approachable and easy to get on with, it is very easy to lose yourself in conversation with such individuals. It is with these personality types that you really need to be on your guard. So lets take a look at the contenders.

The extrovert

Extroverts are very sociable creatures and thrive on interaction. They are comfortable speaking to large audiences, are very open with their thoughts and feelings, and take an enthusiastic approach to most activities. This personality type is easy to get caught up in dialogue with, so you need to be extra cautious about the information you openly reveal when in their intoxicating presence. Enjoy the buzz they create and allow their enthusiasm to radiate through you and if you have an introverted tendency, just bide you time and make an effort to enjoy their vibrant presence.

The entertainer

Just like extroverts, entertainers are sociable, talkative and very energetic people. They love to be the centre of attention and often have an infectious personality. It is very easy to like the entertainer as they have a very down to earth and friendly attitude. When interacting with an entertainer, avoid being overly serious and just allow their positive energy to flow through you. An officer will use this type of personality to lure you into a false sense of security, so beware.

Pam Ann

In using the term 'model', I am not referring to looks. Rather, I am referring to those candidates who seem to be models of perfection. They appear to say and do all the right things, seemingly without a care or worry in the world. They naturally exude charisma and confidence, and have a magnetic personality. Officers will use this personality type for two reasons. The first is so officers can gauge other candidates reactions to their presence, and two, they will be providing an example for others to learn from. In observing these candidates, examine what makes them appear perfect and be appreciative of those traits.

The leader

Natural leaders are instantly recognisable by their innate desire to step up. Their confident, assertive and intelligent character inspires trust in others, while their sensitive, inspiring and sincere side inspires confidence. Officers will often use this approach to test a candidate's ability and willingness to support and encourage their fellow candidates without viewing them as competition. In the presence of a good leader, respect, support and encourage their efforts. Participate and be an active member of their team and you may just join them in the next round.

These are just some of the personality types that you may come across, but there may be many more. So always be on your guard with everyone you come in contact with.

Handling questions and dialogue

Handling a personality type is one thing, but answering their intrusive questions or resisting deadly dialogue is quite another. So here are a few tips that will help you in this most critical part of the process.

Q: So, what do you do for a living?

This question is so common and seemingly innocent that it is easy to get caught out with. If you are between jobs, dislike your current job, or are desperate to find a new job this question can lead to and encourage negative dialogue. When answering this question, just remember to keep the discussion positive and be careful not to reveal too much about your personal circumstances if they are less than ideal.

Q: Don't you just hate interviews?

Let's be honest, unless you are like me and attend them for fun or research purposes, it is unlikely that you will relish attending interviews. However, just as you would attempt to diffuse a negative interview question with a positive response, you should do the same here. So, rather than admit to disliking interviews, you can state that you simply see it as a necessary part of the process in achieving the job that you desire and, therefore, you appreciate its necessity.

Q: This is my seventh attempt. How many interviews have you attended?

If an applicant asks you any questions regarding your previous interview attempts or current interview strategies you really must not divulge such information. You could attempt to change the subject in the first instance or, failing that, you may be polite and state that you would rather not focus on the past as you are trying to remain focused on the present.

Q: I had to take a sickie to attend this damn thing, how did you manage to take time off?

This question has many motives and your best response is a neutral one. Simply state that you have been preparing for this day for some time and have allocated time into your schedule for its purpose. There is no need to say any more.

Q: I want this job because ... What about you?

An honest and passionate response to this question will surely set you apart, so by all means share this passion if you feel it is appropriate to do so. Clearly the lure of travel is not appropriate, but you may be surprised that some individuals still use this line.

Q: My daughter decided to misbehave, today of all days. Do you have children?

This question is trying to elicit further information about your personal life. Rather than divulge this personal information you may choose to ignore it and just empathise by saying " Kids sure do pick their moments don't they? But you've got to love them". You may then attempt to change the subject. Asking follow-up questions will only encourage further dialogue and you will want to avoid this where possible.

Q: Why do we have to sing and dance? Surely this isn't part of our job description

This comment is trying to entice you to speak negatively about a task. This doesn't necessarily have to be about singing and dancing, it could be about any task. Even if you share their viewpoint, remain positive by indicating that you find such challenges fun and are eager to get involved. Nobody will know how you really feel if you don't share it.

Artful dodging

If you encounter a tenacious officer who continues to press your buttons or if you feel backed into a corner at any time, there may be no alternative but to relieve yourself from their presence as soon as possible.

In planning your escape, you will want to make it as seamless and natural as possible so that you can avoid, or at least minimise, causing offence. You could do this during a task or a session break when the individual is conversing with other candidates. This will make it less likely that your disappearance will be noticed. Whatever you do, be sure to have a plan in mind or you risk being left alone and looking like a lost puppy: This surely won't do you any favours.

Sure there will be a risk that a real candidate may feel insulted or upset if they catch on to your disappearing act, however, if your escape is truly justified, then such candidates are not worthy of your concern as they will only bring you down. On the other hand, an officer will at least recognise your ability to distance yourself from negative situations.

Now that you understand what you are up against, it is time to learn how to make yourself unforgettable...

Candidate Profiles

You may be familiar with the following statistics:

- 22,000 applications for 300 openings,
- 15,000 applications per month
- 2,500 applicants turning up to open days
- 1% acceptance rate, etc.

With extreme competition comes high failure rates. In fact, Harvard University has a higher acceptance rate at 4.6% than Delta Airlines who have an acceptance rate of just 1%. (Source: Delta.com)

Of the 150,000 applications Delta received in 2017, only 35,000 (23%) were offered video interviews, followed by a shortlisted 6,000 (17%) in person interviews. In all, fewer than 1,500 (1%) were chosen to become flight attendants. This means that 148,500 applicants were unsuccessful in this selection process.

Of the 400 applicants who turned out to the Emirates open day in Spain, only 7.5% (30 applicants) made it through to a final interview.

While all these statistics are technically correct, they only tell part of the story. Within this lesson we will break down these statistics to see what is really going on and put things back into perspective.

The above numbers are real and typical statistics for cabin crew recruitment and can appear intimidating at first glance. While these numbers are technically correct they only tell part of the story.

The role of cabin crew is glamorised and therefore attracts above average volumes of applicants to the candidate pool. This leads to overinflated numbers and a higher perceived difficulty.

Once we break down the profiles of these applicants, you'll understand how competition for the position is really not as overwhelming as the numbers suggest.

Learning about this volume of applicants and the acceptance rate is intimidating, however, the competition isn't necessarily as overwhelming as the numbers would suggest.

The role of cabin crew is glamorised and therefore attracts more than average volumes of applicants to the candidate pool. It is this candidate pool that directly effects these statistics.

There is one key factor that effects this statistic, this is the 'candidate profile'.

In this lesson, we will take a closer look at the candidate pool. This lesson is designed to bring clarity and a fresh perspective to the statistics surrounding the cabin crew recruitment and selection process in order to reduce overwhelm and any underlying anxiety you may have around the process.

Candidate Profiles

Let's say an airline opens up recruitment and attracts 7000 applicants. Of these 7000 applicants, you'll find a variety of applicants who will fit into five potential profiles, these are:

- Speculators
- Hopefuls
- Unsuitable's
- Glamorisers
- Potentials

Let's take a look at each of these profiles in turn.

Speculators

A speculator is a candidate who just wants a job and will settle for anything that pays the bills. They have most likely seen a vacancy and thought they would take a chance on applying.

Glamorisers

You've no doubt come across a glamoriser or two if you have attended a cabin crew interview. You'll recognise the glamoriser by their idea that being cabin crew is an easy way to get paid to travel the world without much work involved. These candidates are only interested in the perks of the job and their desire is purely at a superficial level.

Hopefuls

The hopefuls make up the vast majority of candidates who will apply for the position. They are the candidates who hope to just 'wing it' without carrying out any prior research, and it shows when they arrive at the assessment day totally unprepared. That's presuming they make it that far.

Unsuitable's

The unsuitable candidates are those that don't meet one or more of the requirements set by the airline. Maybe they lack customer service experience, don't meet the minimum height or reach restrictions, or maybe they simply don't fit in with the corporate culture of that particular airline.

Potentials

And finally, there are the potentials. These are the individuals that airlines seek out in their assessments. These are the 1%. The potentials are those candidates who have a real heartfelt desire to be cabin crew and a passion for the airline. It is those who have done their research, fully understand and meet the requirements of the position, and are willing to work hard for their future employer and passengers.

Note: If you have ever watched a televised singing contest such as American Idol or X Factor, you have been witness to an exaggerated version of these same profiles.

Already in breaking down these profiles you can see and appreciate that the competition is not as high as numbers would have you believe., and that's not even taking into consideration those candidates that don't handle interview pressure well.

It's Subjective

I want you to imagine for a moment that you are communicating with a speculator, hopeful, unsuitable or glamoriser (SHUG). To a SHUG, the interview process will appear to be very difficult indeed, and they will have no problems sharing their tales of woe and misfortune. And, because there are a lot of SHUG's, these tales spread like wildfire from one person to the next, leaving almost everyone with a sense of fear and dread. But these fears are totally unfounded - if you are a 'potential'.

The rumours you hear and the stories your read are all subjective experiences that have no bearing on the realities of the recruitment process, and listening to such opinions and awfulising of the process will only serve to tarnish your mindset and set you up for a self fulfilling prophecy.

The airline selection process is set up to screen out the SHUG's and uncover the potentials. With this in mind, I want you to clear your mind of everything you have heard and read, even forget what may have happened in the past and be willing to start over with a fresh perspective.

You have enrolled onto this program because you are a potential and, throughout each lesson, we're going to help you bring out that potential.

I know that this may seem difficult to comprehend right now, particularly if you have been trying for long periods without success, and I don't intend to make light of your efforts. I myself have suffered through the woes of cabin crew recruitment. I spent 7 long and painful years trying before I was successful in my pursuit.

Before I was offered my first position with Emirates, I too would have told you that the process is difficult because, I'll be honest with you, I was one of the SHUG's. In fact, I fell into two categories, hopeful and unsuitable. But I learned from my failures and then coached myself to success. If I can do it, I know you can too.

As you are here, taking action, I already know you are a potential. So, whatever has happened in the past, however you feel you have performed, however many times you have applied, it doesn't matter. You only need to succeed once. Within this program, you will discover how to highlight your potential and succeed.

Timeline

Cabin crew recruitment can be a lengthy process.

For Middle Eastern Airlines, four to six months, from application to date of joining, is a realistic and consistent timeframe. Three to four of those months mark out practical recruitment procedures, followed by several weeks of processing within the Human Resources department.

Blocks of silence are scattered throughout the entire process as thousands of applicants are screened.

Airline personnel process and screen thousands of applicants during this time, therefore, expect blocks of silence, particularly during the final one to two months.

Students have journaled timeframes shorter than this, though these are rare exceptions.

Emirates (Open Day)	Date
Application submitted	January, 29, 2018
Open day in Beirut	April, 7, 2018
Assessment day	April, 8, 2018

Final interview	April, 10, 2018
Golden Call	April, 23, 2018
Date of joining	June, 1,2018

Emirates (Invite)	Date
Document submission and video interview	January, 30, 2018
Application under review	January, 31, 2018
Invited to attend assessment day	February, 4, 2018
Assessment day	February, 9, 2018
Final interview	February, 14, 2018
Interview complete status	March, 6, 2018
Golden call	April, 29, 2018
Date of joining	June, 10, 2018

Qatar (Open Day)	Date
Open day	April, 21, 2018
Assessment day	April, 22, 2018
Final interview	April, 24, 2018
Access granted to on-boarding zone	May, 24, 2018
Golden Call	June, 10, 2018
Date of joining	July, 27, 2018

Following the successful formal interview, candidates are placed into a holding pool until a spot on their training course becomes available, this could also take several weeks.

For those who are unsuccessful in the process, there is a minimum mandatory waiting period of 6 months before the applicant is allowed to reapply for the same position with the same airline, Some airlines, such as easyJet have a 1 year wait.

There is also the risk that the airline won't be hiring when the candidate next ready to reapply. Emirates seized recruitment of cabin crew for a year during 2017. Virgin Atlantic often only hire every 6-12 months. Southwest only open recruitment every few years.

And the bottom line is that there are not an infinite amount of airlines to choose from so candidates need to be at their best when recruitment drives come around.

No Feedback Loop

With so many stages and a highly selective criteria, unsuccessful applicants often leave the process confused about their elimination. However, due to the sheer volume of applicants, it is impossible for airlines to provide applicants with any followup feedback. Oftentimes this means that applicants don't understand how they can improve their candidacy to be successful in the future, leaving them to repeat the same painful process time and time again.

I myself fell foul to this pattern when I first started out. My own lifecycle lasted 7 years before being successful. Several students I have coached have similar tales of woe.

Debunking the Myths

Before we continue on I feel it is important to address some of the myths that are circulating with regards to appearance.

These myths usually imply that airlines only hire crew who embody perfect figures and harbour model looks. This is, quite frankly, utter nonsense. While there is no denying that airlines require candidates to be well groomed and portray a polished image, this element is usually taken out of context and to the extreme.

For candidates who have been victims of the hidden criteria, and already harbour self-doubts about their appearance, this myth often remains one of the few logical explanations that they can establish. This is often exaggerated further if other attractive candidates are seen to be successful.

Unfortunately, such misconceptions are highly destructive, not only to the candidates who may feel inadequate or self-conscious about their own appearance, but also for those who are blessed with above average appearance. Such candidates are unfairly alienated by candidates who feel intimidated in their presence or, worse still, feel themselves superior, thereby leading them into a false sense of security.

Whatever your appearance concerns, the good news is that there are many simple things you can do to dramatically enhance your outward appearance, and you don't have to resort to surgical intervention.

Okay, now that those myths have been officially debunked, we can press on.

Style Guide: Ladies

Consider: Style

Presence is achieved when you look and feel good, so it is important to wear an outfit that you feel the most confident and powerful in. However, in order to stand out for the right reasons, it is important to achieve balance: Balance between how the outfit makes you feel and what impression it creates.

Your outfit should be thoughtful and demonstrate that you have made an effort. So buy the best quality garnets that you can afford, and be sure they are clean and neatly pressed. The idea is to look business-like, yet stylish.

Tasteful, elegant and sophisticated are good objectives to aim for, and you'll want to avoid appearing flashy or overly sexy. Well-coordinated and tailored separates achieve this perfectly, as does a fitted dress in a conservative style: Conservative implying a modest neckline and appropriate length. A quality tailored jacket is a powerful piece that can tie a look together and create a streamlined and professional appearance.

Avoid heavy patterns, as these can appear overwhelming, and be sure to select wrinkle resistant fabrics, such as wool.

Nothing looks more unprofessional or unprepared than rumpled clothes or wrinkled shirts.

Consider: Colour

Colour is a powerful tool that can dramatically increase your chances of standing out. Used appropriately, colour will help you to convey confidence, express your personality and enhance your complexion. So, consider adding a splash of your favourite colour to your outfit for added pizazz.

How much colour you wear will depend on you. There is not necessarily anything wrong with wearing a red pencil dress provided you have the strength of character to pull it off and the colour is flattering against your complexion. However, such a bold statement piece should not be underestimated and must be worn with caution. If you choose to wear a bold piece, be sure that you have the courage of your convictions because you will certainly be noticed and expectations will be set much higher. You wouldn't want to be noticed for looking extremely uncomfortable or for looking washed out by an unflattering colour.

You don't need to be draped in colour to make an impact. In fact, the safest way to wear colour is to add subtle splashes through your accessories, accents or pop pieces. Subtle accents can bring out the sparkle in your eyes and liven up your outfit, without appearing overwhelming or degrading your professionalism.

Whatever you ultimately decide, a contrasting style will bring a sense of balance to the outfit. For a bold and striking colour, opt for a very conservative cut and for a pale tint, add life by selecting a striking style..

Consider: Shoes

The benefits of wearing heels are obvious. They make your legs look longer, shapelier and more feminine, so it is a good idea to wear them if you feel comfortable to do so. Killer heels may have the added butt lifting effect, however, this is not the look you want to achieve at an interview. Heels should be no higher than 3" and thin soles will appear more professional and elegant than thick platforms.

For those of you who are not used to wearing heels or are on the taller side, 1" inch heels will still provide the benefits of wearing heels without the excess height.

Only wear shoes which are clean and in good condition. Tatty shoes, with scuffed toes or heels will detract from the polished image you are trying to create. Open toes, sling backs and splashes of colour are perfectly acceptable as long as they are tasteful and not overly sexy or decorative fashion styles.

Consider: Hosiery

If wearing a dress or a skirt, pantyhose in plain nude or black are essential for creating a polished and professional image, as they will ensure your legs look perfectly smooth and blemish free. Be sure to select a good quality pair, as they will hug your curves better than cheaper alternatives and will be less likely to create the unsightly wrinkled effect around the knees and ankles. Be sure to spot check them before the interview to ensure that there are no runs or ladders and always have an emergency pair in your handbag for good measure.

Consider: Accessories

Jewellery is a great way to spice up a boring black ensemble, giving it character and pizazz, however, be sure to keep your pieces minimal and conservative. Wear no more than one ring per hand, and one set of earrings, and avoid oversized fashion pieces. Bangles that clink can become distracting and annoying, so it is best to avoid them. A timepiece can be worn, but be sure the style is appropriate and turn off any audible sounds.

Observe caution when wearing an engagement ring or wedding band, as such pieces will draw attention to your private life and will leave you open to discrimination.

Consider: Grooming

Grooming is an essential aspect when presenting a polished image. They are the finishing touches that tie your appearance together. Bitten nails, unsightly blemishes and scruffy hair can undermine even the very best of outfits. So be sure to pay extra special attention to the following areas:

Nails should be clean, neatly trimmed and reasonable in length. Nail polish should match in colour and it is best to avoid charms, glitter and multi-coloured polish.

Use cosmetics to conceal blemishes and enhance your assets, but avoid going over the top. Tastefully applied makeup is the best way to achieve a polished and sophisticated look. A touch of mascara and some eyeliner paired with a dash of lipstick is all that is needed. Remember, you are attending an interview not going out for a night on the town. Refined elegance will work better than dramatic.

Tip: Red lipstick is a favourite among most airlines so wearing it to the interview is a fantastic psychological finishing touch. Be sure to visit a cosmetics counter to find the ideal shade of red for your complexion. The wrong shade will be noticeable as it will wash you out and ruin the effect.

Hair should be neat and well groomed, and outrageous colours or styles should be avoided. Frizzy or loose ends can appear messy so brush and fix them into place if necessary. Freshly trimmed hair will be easier to style and keep looking fresh, so book into the salon if necessary.

If you choose to wear perfume, select a light scent and wear it sparingly. There is nothing more off-putting than an overpowering odour, even a pleasant one.

Visible tattoos and facial piercings are not acceptable. Tattoos will need to be concealed and piercings removed. That applies to multiple earrings too.

Consider: The ultimate advantage

Interviewers need to be able to visualise you in the position, so the very act of looking like you are already cabin crew will create a great psychological advantage.

Now, I am not implying that you find a suit in a matching colour to the airlines' uniform with hat and scarf to match. Sure this would make you stand out, but not for the right reasons. Subtlety is the key to success with this strategy. You're trying to capture the airlines aesthetic appeal, not look like you are attending a fancy dress parade.

The best way to pull this off is to look at the cabin crew who already work for the airline. Is red lipstick a part of the uniform? What are the typical hair grooming styles? Are their corporate colours muted, pale or bold? And what about the corporate culture? Is the airline energetic, carefree and fun loving, or conservative and professional? Understanding these aspects will help you to achieve the most appropriate interview look for each airline.

Injecting a splash of the corporate colour into your accessories is a great touch. Another is to tend to your grooming in the same way you would if offered the position. Understanding the corporate culture will further enable you to tailor your outfit according to the tastes of the airline. If the airline is famous for its fun and carefree corporate culture, you can be sure they will be more accepting of bold colours and unique styling, whereas an airline known for its conservative image may not be.

The effort you put in to this will show and it will be apparent that you have done your research to understand the airline's culture. The psychological impact this one trick can achieve is astonishing and should not be underestimated.

Avoid: Fashion faux pas

If you would like to be taken seriously, you need to avoid the following fatal mistakes.

1. Push up bra and plunging necklines
2. Bare midriff
3. Too much makeup or hair product
4. Unnecessary accessories
5. Wrinkled or unkempt clothes
6. Ill fitting garments
7. Cheap and translucent blouses
8. Scuffed or tatty shoes
9. Short skirt
10. Extremely high heels or large platforms
11. Bitten or over the top nails
12. Strong perfume

Style Guide: Gents

When it comes to looking professional, the options for gents are no doubt limited. Formal business attire is essential for creating a professional, polished and streamlined look, however, when every other male candidate is also wearing business attire, how do you stand out from the crowd? It is the attention you pay to the finer details that will show that you have made an effort, and it is this that will get you noticed.

Consider: Fit & Quality

The key to looking your best in a suit is to pay special attention to fit and quality. A well-tailored suit, in a wrinkle free fabric, will create a polished and professional look that will surely set you apart from the rest. Off the rack suits are a popular choice because they are convenient and inexpensive, however, a ready to wear suit is often the worst option when making a good impression is your top priority. As such, it is advisable to purchase the best quality suit you can afford. A custom tailored suit is the obvious choice, however if finances will not stretch to this, purchase an off the rack suit and have some tailored alterations carried out for an inexpensive alternative.

Whichever option you choose, be sure to pay attention to selecting a good quality fabric. Natural fabrics are far better than synthetic fabrics or blends. In particular, wool, such as merino, cashmere and angora, will offer the best in comfort, wrinkle resistance, and longevity.

Consider: Shirt

A good quality, 100% cotton shirt, with long sleeves is essential for appearing professional and crisp. White, ecru and blue are classic and conservative choices and should be your first choice.

Dark shirts are somewhat taboo as they are often considered a style choice, rather than a professional one. As such, you need to proceed with caution if this is what you feel most comfortable wearing. On the one hand it is important to wear what you feel confident and powerful in, but on the other, it is important to achieve balance: Balance between how the outfit makes you feel and what impression it creates. Airlines are no doubt much more open to personal style choices, however, it is a choice that may not be viewed favourably, no matter how powerful and confident it makes you feel. Therefore, it is far better to play it safe.

When it comes to choosing a collar, remember that it will frame your face. As such, you will want to select a collar that brings balance to your face shape. A wide spread collar will compliment a thin and long face well, while a classic point works better on a round face.

Consider: Pattern & Colour

With regards to colour and pattern, it is best to err on the side of caution. Traditional colours, such as navy blue or charcoal grey, are great alternatives to the standard black, while brown, beige and taupe will appear too casual. If you do decide to wear black, try opting for a subtle pinstripe pattern to break up the monotony and strength of the colour.

Consider: Tie

The tie is an extremely important accessory, as it is often the first thing that a person notices.

Since it frames your face, it is important to consider the colour choice carefully because the wrong colour can suck the sparkle out of your complexion, leaving you looking dull and lifeless. When considering colour, assess how it interacts and enhances your complexion. Does red make your skin look bright, vibrant and well rested? or does it make you look sallow and washed out? Likewise, does blue bring a sparkle to your eyes, or does it make your complexion look muddy and ashen?

Pattern is another factor that needs consideration. Character ties and exotic patterns, while demonstrating personality, are not the ideal interview choice. Instead, opt for subtle stripes, simple designs or block colours for a classic and professional look.

For a strong and confident appeal opt for a larger knot, such as the Pratt or Windsor and aim for a length that falls to the same level as the belt buckle. Tie bars and clips may also be worn to keep the tie in place.

Consider: Shoes & Socks

Shoes should be worn in a style and colour that coordinates with the overall look of your suit. Lace up shoes are the classic and safe option, however, loafers can also be worn if they are suitable. A thin sole will create a more professional image than thick rubber soles.

Nicked heels and scruffy toes will ruin the whole outfit, so invest in a new pair if necessary and never underestimate the importance of a good shoeshine.

Socks should be inconspicuous so they don't draw any attention. As such, they should be dark in colour and long enough to cover your calves so that your flesh is not exposed when seated.

Consider: Accessories

Accessories are finishing touches and should be treated as such. This means that they should remain simple to complement your outfit. Cufflinks may be worn if you are wearing a buttonless shirt, and a leather belt with an understated buckle ought not be forgotten.

While a leather briefcase is unnecessary, a leather portfolio will look much more professional than carrying lots of loose papers.

When it comes to jewellery, the simpler and less of it, the better. One ring and a tasteful wristwatch is all that is necessary to project a professional image.

Consider: Grooming

When it comes to grooming a good haircut and clean-shaven face are essential. A few days prior to the interview, have your hair freshly cut or trimmed and be sure to shave on the morning of the interview. Be careful not to cut yourself and try to prevent razor burn.

Nails are another aspect that is often neglected and underestimated by male candidates. A manicure is an attention to detail that will be noticed and appreciated, so visit a manicurist a few days before the interview.

If you must wear cologne, be sure not to use too much as it can be distracting and suffocating.

Consider: The Ultimate Advantage

Interviewers need to be able to visualise you in the position, so the very act of looking like you are already cabin crew will create a great psychological advantage. Now, I am not implying that you arrive in something too similar to the airlines' uniform; however, it doesn't hurt to capture an element of the industries aesthetic appeal. The one item that captures this look the best is a fitted waistcoat. It is an element often under-utilised, but its stylish appeal works wonders within the airline industry.

Some of you may baulk at this idea, however, it is an element, which will get you noticed. Not only do they create a business-like and streamlined appearance, but it will show that you have made an extra special effort. Take a look at the Virgin Atlantic uniform to get a sense of its style for yourself. If a waistcoat does fit in with your personal style, consider including it in your repertoire.

Avoid: Fashion Faux Pas

If you would like to be taken seriously, you need to avoid the following fatal mistakes.

1. Short sleeves
2. Strong cologne
3. Too much hair product
4. Excessive jewellery
5. Wrinkled or unkempt clothes
6. Ill fitting garments
7. Scuffed or tatty shoes
8. Visible tattoos or piercings
9. Rubber sports watch
10. Bow tie or suspenders
11. Excessive facial hair

Appearance concerns

With all the guidance provided and even some myths debunked, I know there are still some of you who have concerns over your appearance. So let's address this before we continue forward.

For those of you with minor or temporary imperfections, such as the occasional pimple or patch of dry skin, I understand that a spot in the middle of your forehead is not ideal, but it isn't a disaster either. Recruiters are human too and will recognise that this is a temporary imperfection and will not base a hiring decision upon it. Likewise if you have a perceived flaw, such as an unusual face shape, off white teeth or a slightly crooked nose, these are characteristics that make you unique and are highly unlikely to make any sort of impact to the strength of your candidacy. So please stop worrying about extremes and focus your attention on what really matters.

On the other hand, if you do have a real concern, such as rosacea, acne, birthmarks or severely stained teeth, it is unfortunate that such appearance concerns can be cause for discrimination, so it really is worthwhile looking into treatments that may be available to you. With the advances in technology, it would appear that nothing is beyond fixing these days, so there is usually a treatment that will work for you.

For scaring, there are non-evasive laser procedures that can drastically minimise their appearance and for acne, there is medication and lotions. For rosacea, dark circles or birthmarks, you will find medical strength concealers and for stained teeth, cosmetic dentistry or tooth whitening procedures. Whatever path you ultimately decide to pursue, it is important to proceed with safety and due consideration.

In Conclusion

While the advice and guidance given in this chapter may sound obvious, unnecessary and, even, unimportant, it has been my experience that many candidates fail to create an impression because they are either confused or uninformed about the standard of dress expected of them or because they neglect to pay enough attention to the details.

Following this guidance will not only multiply your chances of attracting the interviewers attention, but you will also stand out for having made an extra effort.

In the grand scheme of things, it does not matter how well you are dressed or how much effort you have gone through if the rest of your delivery is poor. So, continue reading and you will discover important steps that will make you truly memorable.

Consider your communication

Because effective communication skills are essential for interview success, it is important to be mindful of how your communication is received. This means that you must consider not only the words you use, but also how your tonality and body language complement or contradict those words.

Consider the following communication guidelines:

Word choice

Words are important because they communicate and convey your message succinctly. So, even at a low 7% accountability, your word choice can mean the difference between a powerful, captivating and influential exchange, and a weak, disempowering and ineffective one.

Action Words

Action words are positive, powerful and directive, and should be used abundantly. Action words include:

Communicated, conveyed, directed, listened, persuaded, arranged, handled and improved.

Filler Words

Filler words are useless and annoying verbal mannerisms such as "you know," "huh," "erm," "kind of," "ummm," and "uh". Besides sounding unprofessional, they also distract attention from the message. Filler words should be avoided at all costs.

Undermining words

Words and phrases such as 'I think,' 'I hope,' 'maybe,' 'sort of,' 'perhaps,' 'I guess,' all undermine your message and credibility by creating the impression that you don't trust your own knowledge or opinion. Eliminating these phrases will drastically improve the quality of any message.

Jargon, slang, and chiches

Specialist terminology and informal expressions can confuse an outside audience. Avoid these where possible, and stick to simple, clear and coherent language.

Vocal Quality

Tonality plays a key role in sending the correct messages. So, if your aim is to project confidence, enthusiasm and expertise, it is important to exercise control and awareness of your tonality throughout your interactions.

Pitch

Pitch refers to the degree of highness and lowness in your voice. A variation in your pitch creates meaning, adds clarity and makes what you are saying more interesting. For instance: A rise in your pitch suggests you are asking a question, which indicates doubt, uncertainty and hesitation. A fall in pitch indicates a statement, which suggests certainty and assurance.

Tempo

Tempo refers to the speed of your voice. If you speak too slowly, you risk losing the interest and attention of your audience. If you speak too fast, others may find you difficult to follow. The key is to maintain a pace, which is fast enough to maintain interest, yet slow enough to be clear.

Volume

Speaking in a loud volume suggests aggression, while a quiet volume indicates shyness and makes it difficult to be heard. The key to determining the appropriate volume is to keep your voice loud enough to be heard, but soft enough to be clear. Modulation of volume can also be introduced to keep your speech interesting and add extra emphasis.

Articulation

Articulation refers to vocal clarity. Regardless of our pitch, tempo, volume and accent, you need to make a conscious effort to enunciate clearly.

Communication Barriers

Barriers to effective communication may arise for a number of reasons. When these barriers do occur, you are forced to become even more effective in your ability to communicate. The strategies below will help overcome some of these more effectively.

Language

If you struggle with the native language of the airline, or have a very strong accent, speak slowly and clearly, ask for clarification and check for understanding, avoid idioms and jargon, use gestures and be specific, listen actively and be patient.

Cultural

Because every culture has its own set of values, beliefs and behaviours, the potential for confusion and misunderstanding is high. Even when we speak the same language, these differences can lead to challenges. To effectively connect with an individual from a culturally different background, it is important to be sensitive and respectful, avoid prejudice and stereotyping, and be aware of using questionable language and gestures.

Gender

Barriers in communication between genders exist primarily because men and women have different communication patterns. To overcome these barriers, it is important to appreciate, learn and understand the different strengths and styles that exist.

While men tend to be more direct and factual, women tend to be indirect and tactful. Men have a preference for reason and logic, are competitive and are interested in power, rank and status. Women are empathetic and feeling oriented. They value relationships and like to build rapport. Men communicate to exchange information and solve problems, while women communicate to share and a build connection.

Emotional

Emotional barriers within an interview situation manifest themselves through fear, shyness or restraint. When we feel distracted by these emotional states, our ability to communicate at an effective level is severely inhibited. We may wrongly interpret the actions and words of others, and may not effectively express our own opinion. We may even stop listening to the other person as our internal dialogue takes over.

To effectively deal with these barriers, it is important to treat the underlying cause of such emotions.

Let your body do the talking

The way you carry yourself, the gestures you use and your facial expressions communicate all sorts of messages. If you appear to lack confidence, seem evasive, or exhibit negative body language it is only natural that the interviewer will want to dig further to find out why your body is contradicting your words. So it is worth learning to control certain aspects so that you can convey the message of a well-balanced, confident individual.

The reason why your body language is so important is that it supports and reinforces what you say. In essence you appear to be exactly what you say you are.

Gestures

We use open gestures when we are feeling confident and relaxed, and are being honest and sincere, therefore, keep your arms unfolded, your legs uncrossed and your palms open. Sitting or standing with your arms crossed will be interpreted as a defensive posture and will give the impression that you are uncomfortable, bored, or have something to hide. Likewise, standing in your hands in your pockets suggests unease.

Touching your nose during the interview is commonly interpreted as an indication of dishonesty, so even if it itches, it is best to grin and bear it. Observe caution if you experience the tendency to rub your neck as this too can be misinterpreted as boredom or unease.

Gesturing can be useful for adding emphasis to what you are saying and, if the movements you employ are subtle and controlled, it is perfectly okay to use gestures to express yourself and endorse your words. For best results, keep any movements below shoulder level, but above the waistline.

Posture

Posture is fundamental to appearing alert, confident and motivated, and yet it is shocking to see how many candidates forget this one simple rule. Take a look around the room next time you attend a group interview and you will see candidates slouching and generally looking bored and inattentive while they wait to be assessed.

I understand that the wait can be long and tiresome, however, it is important that you do not let this happen to you. This is the period when you are being watched very closely and letting your posture relax too much will demonstrate disrespect and give the impression that you lack interest.

To portray the image of a confident and motivated person, adopt an upright and attentive posture that is open, yet relaxed. Keep your chin parallel to the floor, shoulders back and spine straight.

If seated, lean slightly forward with your hands loosely in your lap, or on the table. Place both feet flat on the floor, or cross your ankles. And always be sure to direct your body and your feet towards the interviewer and not at the door, as this will give the impression that you feel uncomfortable and are ready to flee.

If standing, keep your arms loosely at your side or behind your back and plant your feet about 8-10 inches apart. If standing for long periods, place one foot slightly in front of the other to allow you to smoothly and unnoticeably shift weight between your feet.

Your carriage

The way you carry yourself is a powerful indicator of how you feel. To be perceived as confident and professional, walk briskly with an erect posture. Keep your shoulders back, your arms loosely at your side, and chin parallel to the floor.

Facial expressions

Your facial expressions convey a wide range of attitudes, feelings and emotions, and these can have a significant impact on your ability to connect with others. Because of this, it is important to be aware of the story your face is telling and work to convey an attentive, sincere and interested expression.

A positive expression can certainly include a smile, but doesn't necessarily imply its inclusion. In fact, maintaining a constant smile is not only uncomfortable, but it is also completely unnecessary. Instead, an open expression that includes a gentle and understated smile, soft eyes and slightly elevated eyebrows will result in a soft and pleasant expression.

Large smiles should be reserved for introductions and the occasional injection during conversation.

Handshake

Your handshake says a lot about you. A firm handshake conveys confidence, assertiveness and professionalism while a weak, limp handshake suggests shyness and insecurity. A strong, crushing handshake indicates aggression and dominance, and should be avoided.

To perform a professional and confident handshake, follow these simple guidelines:

Before connecting for the handshake establish eye contact, smile and lean slightly forward. As you extend your right hand, keep your hand straight and thumb pointing upwards. When your hands connect engage a firm, but not crushing, grip. Pump one to three times, for a duration of 1-3 seconds, and break away.

Eye Contact

Good eye contact is one of the most important factors of body language. Shifty eyes, or complete avoidance of contact can suggest dishonesty, boredom, rudeness, insecurity or shyness.

If you find eye contact anxiety provoking and uncomfortable, direct your gaze at their eyebrows, forehead, or bridge of the nose. This is not a permanent solution by any means, but it will certainly ease you into the process.

In an attempt to forge eye contact, be aware not to stare as this can indicate aggression and make others feel uncomfortable. To avoid this extreme, lighten your gaze and keep it friendly. This can be achieved by allowing your eyes to go slightly out of focus.

If you have notes, you can temporarily break eye contact as you refer to these, and if there is a second recruitment officer present, this will give you opportunity to break eye contact as you periodically direct your focus back and forth between the two.

Aim to maintain eye contact for 80-90% of the time.

Caution: Smokers

Due to the non-smoking environment on board an aircraft and the fact that you will not be able to step outside for a quickie mid-flight, many airlines now have a strict no smoking policy and will not hire smokers. So if you are partial to a cigarette or two, it is important that you refrain from 'sparking up' at any time before or during the interview, as the smell of smoke will linger on your clothing. Once the interview is over, you may of course have one, but be sure you are well away from the building.

To avoid your interview garments becoming infested by the smell of stale smoke, have your outfit cleaned thoroughly and then keep it zipped up in a suit bag away from your smoking environment. On the day of your interview, be sure to wash thoroughly before you handle it.

Although it is possible to try to conceal the smell of smoke, the effort required and the risks involved are far too great and it simply isn't worth it. The best course of action on the day of the interview is to wear a nicotine patch.

If you find the thought of not smoking for the day too much to bear, temporarily switch over to e-cigarettes, but be sure to use it only within the privacy of the W.C. and never in public view.

So, what should you say if you are asked whether you smoke? Well, this will depend on you. You can of course say no, you could be tactful with the truth and simply state that you have recently given up or you can respond in the affirmative. Whichever answer you choose is your decision, but beware that being honest in this instance may be the quickest way for your resume to hit the rejection pile.

In fact, you will find that many airlines now have this as part of the employment contract, so it is worthwhile considering kicking the addiction in the long term.

Create a Memorable Impression

When faced with hundreds, and possibly thousands, of other candidates, merely creating a good impression just isn't enough. You need to be memorable. The trouble is, very few people know how to truly differentiate themselves from the competition. Most candidates enter the interview in their own little bubble, thinking that they only need to dress well and sell their skills and experience. Unfortunately, this is only a small part of it.

Creating a memorable impression goes far beyond what you wear and how you carry yourself, and even beyond the skills and experience you posses. In fact, it is so rare that only 2% of candidates ever make it through to being hired.

The secret to creating a memorable impression will surprise you in its simplicity, and yet many candidates are unaware that such an advantage even exists, let alone know how to evoke it. They often enter the process only prepared for the hard sell, if they are prepared at all, and end up merely blending in with the rest of the crowd.

Recruiters see this same thing time and time again, so any candidate who is prepared to put in just that little bit of extra effort will naturally stand out, and it is these candidates who, ultimately, get hired.

So what is this mysterious phenomenon and how can you use it to your advantage?

The art of the connection

This technique is actually not mysterious at all. In fact, it is not even a secret. The technique involves creating a connection or, most commonly referred to as, establishing a rapport. Rapport is such a powerful tool, as it is the quickest way to achieve a sensation of familiarity and trust between you and the recruiter. It is so powerful, in fact, that it can even sway the hiring decision in your favour.

Why does this technique work so well? Have you ever met someone for the first time and yet you felt a strong connection, just as if you'd known him or her forever? This is rapport in action. If you can establish this level of rapport with the recruiter or undercover officers, you can be sure they will remember you favourably.

The quickest and easiest way to achieve a connection this strong is through the act of mirroring.

Mirror, mirror

Mirroring is a process whereby you match your communication style, posture and mannerisms to those of another person. It is something you do naturally when you are deep in rapport with another person and is created by a deep feeling of unity. Using it consciously can evoke the sensation that the two of you are very much in sync just as readily as if it had occurred at a subconscious level, only you can be in control and use it to your own advantage.

As a note of caution, mirroring is something that must be done subtly to be effective. As such, it is important not to match every movement and not to react instantly to every change, else your motives will become obvious and the effectiveness of the technique will be lost.

For seamless results, take note of the following guidelines.

Body Language

As you are speaking with the recruiter, make a mental note of how they are sitting or standing, and what they are doing with their hands. Then, subtly mirror their position and gestures. If they are leaning forward, you might lean forward also. If they have their hands clasped on the table, you might do the same.

The best time to mirror a position is when you engage in dialogue. For example: The recruiter leans forward as he or she begins to ask you a question. As you engage in your follow up response, a change in position would appear natural and go completely unnoticed.

Be cautious not to mirror any closed signals, such as crossing your arms, as this will only accomplish a negative connection.

Communication Style

Mirroring a communication style can be done through using similar words or phrases, matching the sensory style, or mimicking the pitch, tempo and volume of their voice.

Words and Phrases

You can make a fantastic psychological impact simply by injecting the recruiter's own terminology and sequence of words into your answers. For example, if the interviewer points out that they are looking for and value a candidate who is 'team spirited', inject the same phrase into your answer. Simply stating that "I work well in a team", or "I am a team player", while implying the same values, will not create the same strong psychological impact as using the interviewers own words.

Pitch, Tempo and Volume

Matching your pitch, tempo and volume to the recruiters speaking style will make you appear in tune to what they are saying. This will speed up the rapport process and greatly improve your chances of creating a favourable impression. Keep pace with the interviewer and assess their basic conversational style. If they have a fast pace, assume the same characteristics. If they are analytical and introspective, slow down your responses to their speed.

Sensory Style

While we all use a mix of the sensory styles: Visual, kinaesthetic and auditory, we tend to have a dominant style that we gravitate towards. If, during the course of the interview, it becomes obvious that the recruiter has a preference towards a particular sensory style, you can adjust your style accordingly to establish a deeper connection.

Visual people use words that reflect their visual style, such as: 'I see what you mean', 'It looks to me like...', 'I imagine that...'

Auditory people use hearing words, such as: 'I hear what you are saying', 'We'll discuss this further', 'I hear you loud and clear'

Kinaesthetic people use action words, such as: 'It feels as if...', 'It slipped my mind', 'I have a solid grasp...'

Next time you are in a public place, observe how people who appear to be closely connected do these same things. You could even try this out for yourself next time you are out for lunch with a close friend or family member. In fact, because this technique can appear uncomfortable and awkward the first time you try it, practicing will, in time, make it almost natural and automatic, and you may even find that your relationships begin to blossom more than usual.

Leading

Leading is an influencing technique that can be used to judge the level of connection. For example: If you feel you have achieved rapport with the recruiter, you could change position or make a gesture to see If the recruiter follows your lead. If this does occur, you can be sure that you have established a strong connection. It the test reveals that the connection is not as strong as you thought, simply go back to mirroring to re-establish and strengthen the connection.

Disconnection

It is important to be perceptive to signs that the recruiter has become disconnected so that you can be proactive in re-establishing the connection.

Before attempting to reconnect, however, it is important to establish the accuracy of your perceptions because you may have simply misread the signal or it could be a by-product of a paranoid imagination. Similarly, the perceived signal may be a momentary motion that has no substance or it may be unrelated to you entirely.

To reliably determine the accuracy of your observation, you first need to scan for clusters of signals that are supportive of your perception. If you observe two or more congruent signals, this is a definite cluster. Next, you can test our connection by attempting to 'lead' (see above). If the recruiter doesn't follow, this is also a sure sign that a disconnection has taken place.

When to use it

During the group stages, you will not have an opportunity to forge any kind of connection with the official recruiters, however, you will be up close and very personal with the undercover team and it is here that you will be focusing much of your attention during these early stages.

The trouble is, how do you know who is undercover and who is a candidate? Unfortunately ,you don't. As such, the only possible way to accomplish this task is to make this same effort with every candidate you meet. While this may seem like an arduous and inefficient task, your efforts will pay off many times over, as you will gain an advantage like no other. In the worst instance, you will come away with a few new friends.

During the latter stages of the final interview, you can refocus your efforts on the official recruiters. This is where the technique will really come into its own and you can use it to its full advantage.

The one type who always gets the job

As you can now see, there is always one type who gets the job offer, but it isn't the best looking one as myths and legend would have you believe. The simple truth is that recruiters hire those individuals that they personally like and feel a connection with.

The biggest mistake most candidates make is that they enter the interview focused only on themselves and miss any opportunity to make a connection. A candidate who makes an effort will not only come across as more genuine and sincere, they will also instantly differentiate themselves from the competition, so it is certainly worthwhile putting the extra effort into perfecting this technique.

Just like old friends

Another trick, which can be used as an adjunct to the previous technique, is to think of the recruiter as a good friend. Now I am not suggesting you take this literally, or you risk appearing too informal and familiar, what I am suggesting is that you enter the interview in a natural and conversational frame of mind.

The point of this technique is to help you relax, but also to assist the interviewer in breaking the ice. Simply initiating some friendly dialogue as you first meet the recruiter will help you to create an aura of a warm and approachable person, but also one who is relaxed and confident. Such a personable approach can help the interviewer feel more comfortable in your presence and will certainly get the interview off to a great start.

Naturally you will want to use common sense here to avoid stepping over the invisible line, however, it is important to remember that most candidates will only be thinking about themselves. The interviewer will appreciate your effort to connect.

The enthusiastic approach

If there is just one more thing that can set one candidate apart from the rest, it is the expression of a sincere passion and enthusiasm for the job, airline and the opportunity. Sadly, many people believe that showing enthusiasm will be mistaken for desperation and, as such, suppress their enthusiasm in favour of the laid back and relaxed approach. The truth is, the laid back approach is often mistaken for indifference or disinterest, and this can severely hinder your chances of success.

Another misconception is that being enthusiastic means that you need to be loaded with energy and bouncing off the walls. This is bordering on excitement, rather than enthusiasm, and is not ideal either. As discussed previously, the idea is to match the tempo of the person you are speaking to, and injecting too much energy can make it difficult for others to relate and connect with you, not to mention exhausting. You can certainly be calm and still be enthusiastic.

So what exactly is enthusiasm and how can you use it appropriately?

Use it appropriately

There are several ways that you can display your enthusiasm. This could be through an eagerness and willingness to learn, your facial expression and smile, an expression of pride in your work, actively listening and asking questions, taking notes and even through your knowledge and research about the opportunity and the airline.

You can also be upfront about your enthusiasm by stating it directly. For instance, when asked "Why do you want to be cabin crew?", speak from the heart as you tell them your personal story and the steps you have been taking to achieve your dream. If you have a sincere passion for meeting people from different cultures, express it. If you have a genuine love for assisting in the comfort of others, use it. If you have been participating in volunteer work to enhance your skills for the position, tell them. This is truly where you will stand head over heels above the run-of-the-mill answers that they hear 95% of the time.

Don't underestimate the power

It sounds simple, and even, superfluous, when compared to tangible skills and experiences, however, do not underestimate the power of honest and sincere enthusiasm. It is contagious and will energise those around you. More importantly, recruiters will pick up on your positive energy and will sense that you will approach the job with vigour.

CORPORATE CULTURE

Corporate culture is a very important aspect that is always being assessed throughout your interactions and involvement in the group tasks. For this reason, you should always assume that no matter how irrelevant a task may appear, there is always an underlying motive for its inclusion, and you can almost always be sure it is being sized up against this important criteria.

Because each airline has a unique style, you will find that each selection process varies in its approach.

If you apply to one airline and find the interview process extremely challenging, it is possible that there is a mis-match with the corporate culture and you may find another selection process very easy and is exactly the reason they are carried out as they are.

So, don't be disheartened if you are having a challenge, you may simply need to adjust your focus or your approach.

Appearance Concerns

With all the guidance provided and even some myths debunked, I know there are still some of you who have concerns over your appearance. So let's address this before we continue forward.

For those of you with minor or temporary imperfections, such as the occasional pimple or patch of dry skin, I understand that a spot in the middle of your forehead is not ideal, but it isn't a disaster either. Recruiters are human too and will recognise that this is a temporary imperfection and will not base a hiring decision upon it. Likewise if you have a perceived flaw, such as an unusual face shape, off white teeth or a slightly crooked nose, these are characteristics that make you unique and are highly unlikely to make any sort of impact to the strength of your candidacy. So please stop worrying about extremes and focus your attention on what really matters.

On the other hand, if you do have a real concern, such as rosacea, acne, birthmarks or severely stained teeth, it is unfortunate that such appearance concerns can be cause for discrimination, so it really is worthwhile looking into treatments that may be available to you. With the advances in technology, it would appear that nothing is beyond fixing these days, so there is usually a treatment that will work for you.

For scaring, there are non-evasive laser procedures that can drastically minimise their appearance and for acne, there is medication and lotions. For rosacea, dark circles or birthmarks, you will find medical strength concealers and for stained teeth, cosmetic dentistry or tooth whitening procedures. Whatever path you ultimately decide to pursue, it is important to proceed with safety and due consideration.

In Conclusion

While the advice and guidance given in this chapter may sound obvious, unnecessary and, even, unimportant, it has been my experience that many candidates fail to create an impression because they are either confused or uninformed about the standard of dress expected of them or because they neglect to pay enough attention to the details.

Following this guidance will not only multiply your chances of attracting the interviewers attention, but you will also stand out for having made an extra effort.

In the grand scheme of things, it does not matter how well you are dressed or how much effort you have gone through if the rest of your delivery is poor. So, continue reading and you will discover important steps that will make you truly memorable.

Create a Memorable Impression

Caution: Smokers

Due to the non-smoking environment on board an aircraft and the fact that you will not be able to step outside for a quickie mid-flight, many airlines now have a strict no smoking policy and will not hire smokers. So if you are partial to a cigarette or two, it is important that you refrain from 'sparking up' at any time before or during the interview, as the smell of smoke will linger on your clothing. Once the interview is over, you may of course have one, but be sure you are well away from the building.

To avoid your interview garments becoming infested by the smell of stale smoke, have your outfit cleaned thoroughly and then keep it zipped up in a suit bag away from your smoking environment. On the day of your interview, be sure to wash thoroughly before you handle it.

Although it is possible to try to conceal the smell of smoke, the effort required and the risks involved are far too great and it simply isn't worth it. The best course of action on the day of the interview is to wear a nicotine patch.

If you find the thought of not smoking for the day too much to bear, temporarily switch over to e-cigarettes, but be sure to use it only within the privacy of the W.C. and never in public view.

So, what should you say if you are asked whether you smoke? Well, this will depend on you. You can of course say no, you could be tactful with the truth and simply state that you have recently given up or you can respond in the affirmative. Whichever answer you choose is your decision, but beware that being honest in this instance may be the quickest way for your resume to hit the rejection pile.

In fact, you will find that many airlines now have this as part of the employment contract, so it is worthwhile considering kicking the addiction in the long term.

Stand Out

When faced with hundreds, and possibly thousands, of other candidates, merely creating a good impression just isn't enough. You need to be memorable. The trouble is, very few people know how to truly differentiate themselves from the competition. Most candidates enter the interview in their own little bubble, thinking that they only need to dress well and sell their skills and experience. Unfortunately, this is only a small part of it.

Creating a memorable impression goes far beyond what you wear and how you carry yourself, and even beyond the skills and experience you posses. In fact, it is so rare that only 2% of candidates ever make it through to being hired.

The secret to creating a memorable impression will surprise you in its simplicity, and yet many candidates are unaware that such an advantage even exists, let alone know how to evoke it. They often enter the process only prepared for the hard sell, if they are prepared at all, and end up merely blending in with the rest of the crowd.

Recruiters see this same thing time and time again, so any candidate who is prepared to put in just that little bit of extra effort will naturally stand out, and it is these candidates who, ultimately, get hired.

So what is this mysterious phenomenon and how can you use it to your advantage?

The art of the connection

This technique is actually not mysterious at all. In fact, it is not even a secret. The technique involves creating a connection or, most commonly referred to as, establishing a rapport. Rapport is such a powerful tool, as it is the quickest way to achieve a sensation of familiarity and trust between you and the recruiter. It is so powerful, in fact, that it can even sway the hiring decision in your favour.

Why does this technique work so well? Have you ever met someone for the first time and yet you felt a strong connection, just as if you'd known him or her forever? This is rapport in action. If you can establish this level of rapport with the recruiter or undercover officers, you can be sure they will remember you favourably.

The quickest and easiest way to achieve a connection this strong is through the act of mirroring.

Mirror, mirror

Mirroring is a process whereby you match your communication style, posture and mannerisms to those of another person. It is something you do naturally when you are deep in rapport with another person and is created by a deep feeling of unity. Using it consciously can evoke the sensation that the two of you are very much in sync just as readily as if it had occurred at a subconscious level, only you can be in control and use it to your own advantage.

As a note of caution, mirroring is something that must be done subtly to be effective. As such, it is important not to match every movement and not to react instantly to every change, else your motives will become obvious and the effectiveness of the technique will be lost.

For seamless results, take note of the following guidelines.

Body Language

As you are speaking with the recruiter, make a mental note of how they are sitting or standing, and what they are doing with their hands. Then, subtly mirror their position and gestures. If they are leaning forward, you might lean forward also. If they have their hands clasped on the table, you might do the same.

The best time to mirror a position is when you engage in dialogue. For example: The recruiter leans forward as he or she begins to ask you a question. As you engage in your follow up response, a change in position would appear natural and go completely unnoticed.

Be cautious not to mirror any closed signals, such as crossing your arms, as this will only accomplish a negative connection.

Communication Style

Mirroring a communication style can be done through using similar words or phrases, matching the sensory style, or mimicking the pitch, tempo and volume of their voice.

Words and Phrases

You can make a fantastic psychological impact simply by injecting the recruiter's own terminology and sequence of words into your answers. For example, if the interviewer points out that they are looking for and value a candidate who is 'team spirited', inject the same phrase into your answer. Simply stating that "I work well in a team", or "I am a team player", while implying the same values, will not create the same strong psychological impact as using the interviewers own words.

Pitch, Tempo and Volume

Matching your pitch, tempo and volume to the recruiters speaking style will make you appear in tune to what they are saying. This will speed up the rapport process and greatly improve your chances of creating a favourable impression. Keep pace with the interviewer and assess their basic conversational style. If they have a fast pace, assume the same characteristics. If they are analytical and introspective, slow down your responses to their speed.

Sensory Style

While we all use a mix of the sensory styles: Visual, kinaesthetic and auditory, we tend to have a dominant style that we gravitate towards. If, during the course of the interview, it becomes obvious that the recruiter has a preference towards a particular sensory style, you can adjust your style accordingly to establish a deeper connection.

Visual people use words that reflect their visual style, such as: 'I see what you mean', 'It looks to me like...', 'I imagine that...'

Auditory people use hearing words, such as: 'I hear what you are saying', 'We'll discuss this further', 'I hear you loud and clear'

Kinaesthetic people use action words, such as: 'It feels as if...', 'It slipped my mind', 'I have a solid grasp...'

Next time you are in a public place, observe how people who appear to be closely connected do these same things. You could even try this out for yourself next time you are out for lunch with a close friend or family member. In fact, because this technique can appear uncomfortable and awkward the first time you try it, practicing will, in time, make it almost natural and automatic, and you may even find that your relationships begin to blossom more than usual.

Leading

Leading is an influencing technique that can be used to judge the level of connection. For example: If you feel you have achieved rapport with the recruiter, you could change position or make a gesture to see If the recruiter follows your lead. If this does occur, you can be sure that you have established a strong connection. It the test reveals that the connection is not as strong as you thought, simply go back to mirroring to re-establish and strengthen the connection.

Disconnection

It is important to be perceptive to signs that the recruiter has become disconnected so that you can be proactive in re-establishing the connection.

Before attempting to reconnect, however, it is important to establish the accuracy of your perceptions because you may have simply misread the signal or it could be a by-product of a paranoid imagination. Similarly, the perceived signal may be a momentary motion that has no substance or it may be unrelated to you entirely.

To reliably determine the accuracy of your observation, you first need to scan for clusters of signals that are supportive of your perception. If you observe two or more congruent signals, this is a definite cluster. Next, you can test our connection by attempting to 'lead' (see above). If the recruiter doesn't follow, this is also a sure sign that a disconnection has taken place.

When to use it

During the group stages, you will not have an opportunity to forge any kind of connection with the official recruiters, however, you will be up close and very personal with the undercover team and it is here that you will be focusing much of your attention during these early stages.

The trouble is, how do you know who is undercover and who is a candidate? Unfortunately ,you don't. As such, the only possible way to accomplish this task is to make this same effort with every candidate you meet. While this may seem like an arduous and inefficient task, your efforts will pay off many times over, as you will gain an advantage like no other. In the worst instance, you will come away with a few new friends.

During the latter stages of the final interview, you can refocus your efforts on the official recruiters. This is where the technique will really come into its own and you can use it to its full advantage.

The one type who always gets the job

As you can now see, there is always one type who gets the job offer, but it isn't the best looking one as myths and legend would have you believe. The simple truth is that recruiters hire those individuals that they personally like and feel a connection with.

The biggest mistake most candidates make is that they enter the interview focused only on themselves and miss any opportunity to make a connection. A candidate who makes an effort will not only come across as more genuine and sincere, they will also instantly differentiate themselves from the competition, so it is certainly worthwhile putting the extra effort into perfecting this technique.

Just like old friends

Another trick, which can be used as an adjunct to the previous technique, is to think of the recruiter as a good friend. Now I am not suggesting you take this literally, or you risk appearing too informal and familiar, what I am suggesting is that you enter the interview in a natural and conversational frame of mind.

The point of this technique is to help you relax, but also to assist the interviewer in breaking the ice. Simply initiating some friendly dialogue as you first meet the recruiter will help you to create an aura of a warm and approachable person, but also one who is relaxed and confident. Such a personable approach can help the interviewer feel more comfortable in your presence and will certainly get the interview off to a great start.

Naturally you will want to use common sense here to avoid stepping over the invisible line, however, it is important to remember that most candidates will only be thinking about themselves. The interviewer will appreciate your effort to connect.

The enthusiastic approach

If there is just one more thing that can set one candidate apart from the rest, it is the expression of a sincere passion and enthusiasm for the job, airline and the opportunity. Sadly, many people believe that showing enthusiasm will be mistaken for desperation and, as such, suppress their enthusiasm in favour of the laid back and relaxed approach. The truth is, the laid back approach is often mistaken for indifference or disinterest, and this can severely hinder your chances of success.

Another misconception is that being enthusiastic means that you need to be loaded with energy and bouncing off the walls. This is bordering on excitement, rather than enthusiasm, and is not ideal either. As discussed previously, the idea is to match the tempo of the person you are speaking to, and injecting too much energy can make it difficult for others to relate and connect with you, not to mention exhausting. You can certainly be calm and still be enthusiastic.

So what exactly is enthusiasm and how can you use it appropriately?

Use it appropriately

There are several ways that you can display your enthusiasm. This could be through an eagerness and willingness to learn, your facial expression and smile, an expression of pride in your work, actively listening and asking questions, taking notes and even through your knowledge and research about the opportunity and the airline.

You can also be upfront about your enthusiasm by stating it directly. For instance, when asked "Why do you want to be cabin crew?", speak from the heart as you tell them your personal story and the steps you have been taking to achieve your dream. If you have a sincere passion for meeting people from different cultures, express it. If you have a genuine love for assisting in the comfort of others, use it. If you have been participating in volunteer work to enhance your skills for the position, tell them. This is truly where you will stand head over heels above the run-of-the-mill answers that they hear 95% of the time.

Don't underestimate the power

It sounds simple, and even, superfluous, when compared to tangible skills and experiences, however, do not underestimate the power of honest and sincere enthusiasm. It is contagious and will energise those around you. More importantly, recruiters will pick up on your positive energy and will sense that you will approach the job with vigour.

Corporate Culture

Corporate culture is a very important aspect that is always being assessed throughout your interactions and involvement in the group tasks. For this reason, you should always assume that no matter how irrelevant a task may appear, there is always an underlying motive for its inclusion, and you can almost always be sure it is being sized up against this important criteria.

Because each airline has a unique style, you will find that each selection process varies in its approach.

If you apply to one airline and find the interview process extremely challenging, it is possible that there is a mis-match with the corporate culture and you may find another selection process very easy and is exactly the reason they are carried out as they are.

So, don't be disheartened if you are having a challenge, you may simply need to adjust your focus or your approach.

Boost your Candidacy

Ulterior motives

It is true to say that job applications are primarily used to collect data for the purpose of evaluating skills, qualifications, employment history and motives, however, what most individuals don't realise is that there is an ulterior motive.

From the airline's perspective, the form serves a number of other important purposes, namely: To evaluate the applicant's literacy, ability to follow instructions, penmanship and communication skills. Recruiters will be looking or any excuse to thin the pack, so a careless applicant, or one who doesn't follow instructions, will quickly disqualify themselves, and the recruiter will not take the time to decipher what is written on it.

Unlike resume's, which are unique to each individual, the standardised format of an application form allows selectors to quickly peruse and compare each form, and it is easy to see which candidates have made an effort and those who haven't.

Consider the following examples.

> I CURRENTLY WORK AS A FREELANCE HAIRDRESSER AND HAVE WORKED IN CLIENT FACING ROLES FOR MORE THAN 8 YEARS. I AM LOOKING FOR A CHANGE IN MY LIFE DIRECTION AND FEEL THAT A CAREER AS CABIN CREW WILL GIVE ME THIS.

> I curently work as freelance hairdresser & have worked in client facing roles fore more than 8 years. I am looking for a change in my life direction and feel that that a career as cabin crew will give me this.

The first example is tidy and creates a positive impression of the candidate. Meanwhile, the second example is messy, full of typos and barely legible. It is clear that the candidate jumped straight in without planning. Hardly a positive first impression.

To ensure this doesn't happen to your application form, take note of the following guidelines.

Important guidelines
Before you begin

- Read through the form to familiarise yourself with the questions and any specific instructions
- Gather materials: Black pens, a pencil and eraser
- Gather the necessary information:
- Personal details: Passport, contact information, vital statistics
- Education and training information: Qualifications, dates, results
- Employment History: Names, addresses, key dates
- Plan what you want to write in each section, taking note of the space available

Completing the form

- Set aside sufficient time and minimise distractions
- Re-read the instructions as you work on each section
- Write clearly and neatly: Block capitals are tidy and easy to read
- Keep your text within the space provided (Practice on a blank sheet of paper if you are unsure of the space available)
- Answer every question and use 'Not Applicable' or 'N/A' where questions are not relevant to you
- Keep the tone positive and be mindful not to volunteer negative information

- Be concise and avoid continuations on separate sheets of paper. If unavoidable, remember to clearly state your name and detail which part of the application form it is linked to

Finishing off

- If time permits, walk away for a few hours and return with a fresh pair of eyes
- Finish off with a quick proofread and make any necessary adjustments if there are typos, grammatical errors and inaccuracies
- If time permits, make a copy of the final form for future reference

Mailing off the form

- Select an envelope that is large enough not to require any folding of the form
- Address the envelope correctly and apply the correct postage
- Send it off before the closing date

Stretching the truth

If you are thinking about padding out your application form in order to increase your chances of being hired, you wouldn't be the first. Many candidates are tempted to stretch the truth either to gain a favourable advantage or as a means to cover undesirable facts.

Airlines are savvy to this idea and often verify the details you include within it. So, beware that exaggerations and untruths can come back to haunt you if you are quizzed about them at the interview, or later in employment. If you are caught, any future you may have had with the airline will be devastated.

What are the chances of your information being verified? 100%. This is an industry that places high importance on security, and an airline is not going to take any risks with providing airside passes to just anyone. Your references will be contacted and your background checked, so be safe and don't take any unnecessary risks. There are many things you can do to boost your candidacy and minimise imperfections, and it just isn't worth the risk.

Minimise a fragmented work history

A fragmented work history will give the impression of a job hopper and will raise serious doubts about your commitment. Whether the assumption is true or not, it surely doesn't present a favourable impression,

Whatever the reason, whether you have held temporary agency contracts, have been struggling to find something that you can feel committed to, or have simply been trying to gain a more rounded skill-set, it is important to draw attention away from it so that you can avoid any negative and rash assumptions being made.

Here are some options:

Eliminate

Where a position holds little or no relevance, was held only briefly, is dated, or was only held part time, you may be able to safely exclude it from your application. Beware that you should only do this if doing so will not create damaging gaps.

Spring into summer

Instead of listing specific dates for summer jobs, you can simply state Summer 20xx to Spring 20xx.

Consecutive combining

Where several similar consecutive jobs appear or were provided by the same agency, you can combine them into one chunk, for example:

2004–2006 Receptionist

Aztec Hotel & Spa, Bloomfields Leisure, Trina's Hair & Beauty Salon

2001–2003 Customer service manager

Multi-national business agency

Fill gaps in employment

If you have gaps in your employment history, you may be asked to elaborate on these. Whatever your reasons: whether it was for maternity leave, study or a travel break, you need to observe caution about revealing too much about your personal circumstances. Revealing that you had taken maternity leave will highlight your parental status and could be used as a tool to discriminate against you.

If you were doing anything during the gaps, paid or unpaid, inserting them in place of the gap will add much needed bulk and minimise the appearance of the gaps, for example:

| Summer 2004–Spring 2005 | Travelled around Europe |
| July 2001–November 2001 | Study break |

Never admit to being fired

When it comes to lying, there is one exception to the rule and that is if you have a termination on your record. The recruiters will not care if the termination was unjust, unfair or has a good explanation, a termination is a big red flag and will mark the end of your interview so you need to do everything you can to avoid disclosing it.

In the first instance, you may choose to omit the information. Omitting details is not the same as telling an outright lie or making a false statement. When asked for reference details, simply choose another referee.

If you have just been fired from your most recent employment, they will not know unless you tell them. So you could mark your employment to present and leave it at that. If asked if they can call your employer for a reference, it would not raise any eyebrows if you respectfully decline due to your ongoing employment.

The third option is to take proactive measures to have the termination designation changed. If the termination occurred some time ago, it is more likely that the employer will be open to changing the designation if you accept responsibility and demonstrate a sincere regret for the situation. Simply advise them that the termination is damaging your chances of gaining employment and you would like the designation changed to something neutral, such as laid off or resigned.

If you would feel uncomfortable or unethical to omit such a detail and would prefer to take accountability for what happened, be sure to downplay the termination on your application form by simply stating 'will explain at interview'. You will have some damage control to contend with, so remember to accept the mistake, don't blame others and don't make any excuses. Stick to the facts, point out what went wrong and what you have learned from the experience.

Whichever route you take, there is a risk. Either you not be hired by admitting to the termination or you may not be hired because you did not disclose it and were caught out. The decision has to be yours.

Age discrimination

Unfortunately, age discrimination does occur within the airline industry, so you need to take proactive measures to you protect yourself if you are a mature candidate. Lengthy employment is often a clear indication of your age, as are graduation dates. In this instance, you may consider omitting dates and providing only a partial employment history. While this may only provide a temporary level of protection, at least you can buy yourself some time to demonstrate your suitability for the position before it comes to light.

Communicate your suitability

The most important aspect of your application form is that you must communicate your suitability for the position clearly by highlighting the skills and experience that are relevant and transferable. Using a selection of key words that are often used to describe the cabin crew position will achieve this.

For example, a salon receptionist may include the following:

- Delivered the highest level of customer service
- Ensured customer comfort
- Provided a friendly and professional service

- Assisted with enquiries and resolved complaints

These short action statements identify customer service experience and the ability to handle specific responsibilities that are required of cabin crew. It would be clear to any airline that this candidate has the necessary experience and is adequately qualified for the position.

Use action phrases

When describing your duties, three to five action phrases have a better impact than complete sentences or generic job descriptions. Consider the following examples:

Complete sentence

'As a call centre officer, I answer customer queries and complaints over the telephone'

Action statement

'Addressed customer queries and resolved complaints'

The former example has a passive tone and is unnecessarily wordy, whereas the latter example uses an active and punchy tone. Such statements will grab the attention of the reader much more readily than lengthy paragraphs.

Leverage your leisure interests

Recreational interests create depth and humanises your character. A targeted list, which focuses on relevant skills, will form an immediate and positive impression. Such interests also serve as excellent sources of additional skills and experiences, which can be advantageous if you lack relevant experience in a work environment.

Generalised list statements such as: 'reading, watching television, sport and socialising' should be avoided, as should unprofessional statements such as: 'I enjoy spending time with my mates, hitting the town and going out on the razz".

Take a look at the following example:

"I have been keen on netball for as long as I can remember and am an active member of my local netball club where I have been captain of the team for 3 years. I have an active interest in nature, and regularly get involved with and manage conservation assignments. To relax, I attend yoga and meditation classes, which help to keep me focused and relieve any build-up of stress.'

This statement gives an immediate impression of someone who is balanced and committed. Their interests highlight several admirable qualities such as team spirit and leadership, and it also details their methods of stress management. A recruitment office would form a positive impression of the candidate based on a statement such as this.

Be mindful about over-indulging in your leisure interests, as the recruiter may get the impression that your hobbies will take priority over your work.

The power of a personal statement

At the end of most application forms, you will be presented with some form of additional information box. This box may simply state 'Additional Information', or it could be more specific, such as: Please state your reason for applying and why you feel you are suited to the position of cabin crew?

Essentially, this is an opportunity to sell yourself and should never remain blank. Use it to provide a power statement that summarises your experience, highlights your key skills, and shares your motives all within a few short paragraphs.

Consider the following example:

'As you will note, I have eight years experience within the retail industry. Within which, I have built extensive customer relations, team working and supervisory experience, which has also greatly enhanced my communication and interpersonal skills.

With these skills and experiences, combined with my passion for the airline industry, my motivation to succeed, strong attention to detail, and unparalleled work ethic, I am confident that I will make a positive contribution to the airline and excel as a member of the Fly High cabin crew team."

The above example is concise. It focuses on what the candidate can offer the airline, rather than what the airline can offer the candidate, and it showcases skills and experiences that are an asset for a cabin crew position.

Highlight career progression

If you have remained with an employer for several years, but have progressed through the ranks, you can make your progression more obvious by listing each position as you would a new job.

List your awards

Outstanding excellence will show commitment and talent, so if you have achieved any awards through your activities, be sure to list them. Make sure the achievements are recent though, as outdated awards may give the impression that you haven't achieved anything since.

Get permission from referees

Always get permission from the person(s) you state as your referee(s) and give them a copy of your application form or resume to help them write a relevant reference that highlights your most important points.

Resume Guidance

Influence the direction of the interview

Because the recruiters will have no information about you beyond this document, it will be a major influence in the nature and direction of the interview. This allows an element of predictability and makes it a very powerful document indeed.

With such a valuable tool at your disposal, it is important that it represents the best you have to offer. If your resume is strong, it will focus the recruiter's questioning on information that presents your image strongly. The following guidelines will help you achieve this.

Colour

Use colour sparingly. Black text, with a consistent injection of colour for the headings will make your resume more pleasing to the human eye. Colour paper should be avoided as scanning or photocopying will be problematic.

Length

For this type of position, one or two pages is ideal. However, don't be constrained by this advice if doing so will mean that you have to squeeze your data in and use a tiny 8 point font, If you do find your resume going beyond this quota, be sure that it isn't being filled with unnecessary, unfocused or excessive detail.

Single or double sided?

Double sided prints are harder to photocopy and risk show through. Stick to single sided prints for a cleaner look.

Staples

Never staple your sheets together. Staples are inconvenient for the employer if they need to photocopy or scan your resume, plus the reviewer may want to view the pages side by side. A traditional paper clip is acceptable.

Identification

Be sure all of the pages include your name and page numbers so they can be easily reconnected should they become separated.

OCR technology

To facilitate more efficient processing of resumes, some larger airlines use a computerised tracking system. This system uses OCR (Optical Character Recognition) technology, whereby incoming resumes are scanned as a graphic image, converted back into text, read and added to the database.

With this in mind, it is important to write and format your resume in such a way that it can be successfully processed by these sophisticated systems. In this instance, the following guidelines apply:

The system scans your resume for keywords that indicate your skills, qualifications and experience. Following the scan, a score will be awarded based on the number of 'hits'. From this score, the system will either generate a letter of invitation, or a letter of rejection.

To ensure a high score, and an invitation letter, it is essential that you inject as many keywords as possible throughout your resume. The following highlighted keywords are the most widely scanned for:

- Good communication and interpersonal skills
- A confident and friendly personality
- Extensive customer service experience
- Confidence in dealing with a range of people
- The ability to work effectively in a team

- Ability to handle difficult customers firmly and politely
- Ability to stay calm, composed and focused under pressure
- The ability to be tactful and diplomatic, but also assertive when necessary

Action verbs

Action verbs express action. They are positive, powerful and directive, and should be used abundantly throughout your résumé.

Notice how using direct action verbs make the sentence powerful:

"As a hairdresser, I consulted with clients and provided advice"

Format

There are three basic resume formats:

- Chronological
- Functional
- Combination

CHRONOLOGICAL

The chronological résumé highlights the dates, places of employment and job titles, having employment and education detailed first.

Ideal For:

- Demonstrating career progression
- If you want to highlight your career within the airline industry

Avoid if:

- You have large gaps in employment or a chequered history
- Are going through a major career change

Here is a typical outline of a chronological format:

- Personal Information
- Career Summary
- **Detailed Career History (defining section)** *(In Reverse Chronological Order)*
- Additional Skills & Achievements

- Education & Qualifications
- Interests & Hobbies
- References

The focus with this format is on your career history, so you will display the employer, date from and to, job title and a breakdown of your responsibilities starting from the most recent first.

FUNCTIONAL

A functional résumé focuses on skills and achievements and uses functional headings, such as Sales, Customer Service and Teamwork, instead of the chronological employment data.

Ideal for:

- Downplaying an extreme career change
- Concealing large gaps in employment or a chequered employment history.
- To highlight a relevant skill set

Avoid if:

- You are a recent graduate or are lacking experience
- You lack relevant or transferable skills

Here is a typical outline of a functional format:

- Personal Information
- Career Objective
- Career Summary
- **Key Skills** (*Using functional headings such as sales, managerial, customer service, etc*)
- **Brief Education & Employment History**
- Interests & Hobbies
- References

The format focuses more on key skills, so break those down into strong areas of interest to the airline, and elaborate on how these have been demonstrated. Rather than a detailed breakdown of your career and education, you will want to include just a brief overview.

COMBINATION

The combination résumé, is a combination of the chronological and functional formats.

Ideal for:

- Showcasing a relevant and developed skill set
- Making a career change
- Highlighting lots of relevant expertise

Here is a typical outline of a combination format:

- Personal Information
- Career Objective
- Career Summary
- **Key Skills** (*Using functional headings such as sales, managerial, customer service, etc*)
- **Detailed Career History** (*In Chronological Order*)
- Education & Qualifications
- Interests & Hobbies
- References

With this format, you will include both the key skills and a detailed career history. Key skills will come first, with experience directly following.

Outline

Applicant information

At the beginning of the résumé, include your name, your home mailing address, your telephone number(s), and your e-mail address. If you have both temporary and permanent addresses, include them both.

Objective statement (Optional)

When writing your objective statement, there are four key points to keep in mind that will make it smoking hot.

- Be specific
- Focus on benefits you offer
- Keep it short
- Make it relevant to the position

USE AIRLINE KEYWORDS

Here is where the research you conducted in the first module will begin to pay off.

To make your objective even more powerful and specific, you are going to insert the airline's own person specification keywords right into your objective. This is highly targeted and makes it easier to select qualities that the airline considers most valuable.

EXAMPLES

A hard working and reliable customer service advisor looking to apply 3+ years of customer facing experience and excellent interpersonal skills to a cabin crew role within Fly High Airlines.

Seeking a cabin crew position with Fly High Airlines where my customer relations experience and warm interpersonal style can be effectively used to provide passengers with a first class and welcoming experience.

Friendly and enthusiastic nurse looking to bring excellent interpersonal and communication skills, and 4+ years of experience within the health care industry to the role of cabin crew within Fly High Airlines.

A professional and reliable travel operator with 5+ years of experience within a customer facing and teamwork oriented role looking to bring an enthusiastic and personable nature to the role of cabin crew with Fly High Airlines.

Key skills (Optional)

The key skills section provides a fantastic opportunity for you to quickly express your suitability for the role and show what transferable skills you will bring. It will also bulk out your résumé with the keywords that will be picked up by OCR scanning technology (More on this later).

Key skills can be those gained through your work experience or hobbies, even though your studies and voluntary placements. This is why they are so valuable, especially if you have a short career history.

Key skills fit into the following three distinct categories:

- Transferable skills
- Aptitude skills
- Job-related skills

TRANSFERRABLE SKILLS

Transferable skills are generally learned skills and include those that can be picked up from your hobbies and personal interests, volunteer work, employment or education and can be transfered across to any industry or position. The transferable skills airlines are interested in include:

- Teamwork
- Time management
- Customer service
- Foreign languages
- Decision making
- Problem solving
- Leadership and management

APTITUDE SKILLS

Aptitude skills tend to overlap transferable skills, however, aptitude skils are those that are inherited as part of your character. Aptitude skills could include:

- Initiative
- Interpersonal skills
- Communication
- Adaptability
- Motivation
- Postive nature
- Tenacity
- Loyalty
- Friendly / Sociable
- Logical

JOB RELATED SKILLS

Job related skills are those that are specific to an industry. The key here is to find relatable skills within that industry that could become transferable. For instance:

- Hairdresser > Customer service
- Tour guide > Public speaking
- Nurse > First aid and empathy
- Travel agent > Currency conversion
- Call centre op > Handling complaints
- Interior designeer > Managing people
- Self employed > Self starter
- Technical support > Explain complex information clearly

Whatever jobs you have held, look for a transferrable and relatable skill.. Highlight those as much as possible. Suddenly a seemingly irrelevant position can be seen as highly valuable.

EXAMPLE STATEMENTS

Once you have picked out 4 or 5 key skills, elaborate with short statements that provide insight to how you have applied these in the past. Here are some examples:

Extensive Interpersonal Skills

Working as a personal trainer for the past 5 years has given me first hand experience working very closely with people from all backgrounds and of all ages.

Team Spirited and ability to use my own initiative

Working as a waitress has given me an opportunity to develop my team working skills to a high standard, but it has also taught me to use my own initiative when working under pressure.

Problem Solver

Working as a freelance designer has given me an opportunity to develop finely tuned problem solving skills. I am able to think fast on my feet and deal effectively with challenges that create a positive outcome.

Strong customer service skills

As part of my job being a call centre handler, I have had the opportunity to develop a very rounded skill set that enables me to be empathetic to the customer, while also having the company interests in mind in order to ensure the best possible outcome for all concerned.

Employment history

Employment history should be displayed starting with your most recent position, working backwards and include the following elements:

- Name of employer
- Position held
- Period of employment
- Duties performed
- Achievements

DESCRIBING DUTIES

When describing your duties, there are three key points to bear n mind, these are:

- Use short phrases
- Make it relatable
- Focus on results

ACTION PHRASES

Action phrases offer greater impact than compete sentences or generic job descriptions because being short and punchy allows for easy scanning. Here are some examples of such phrases:

- Supervised and trained a team of four junior-level stylists
- Manage and maintain a customer base of over 100 clients
- Maintain up to date records of customer accounts
- Ensure customer comfort and satisfaction
- Assist with enquiries and resolve complaints

RELATABLE

As we discussed earlier, the points of the job you want to extract and highlight, are those that are relatable to the position of cabin crew.

Notice how breaking down the job of an interior designer below can appear totally different, depending on the words we use. Same job, different outcome and impression.

Avoid this

- Develop & design interior concepts
- Consider materials and analyse costs
- Source products
- Survey building

- Blah, blah, blah...

Do this

- Discuss client requirements
- Communicate & negotiate with suppliers
- Collaborate with a team of designers, architects and suppliers
- Supervise contractors to ensure the customer requirements are met

While the first example has no relevant keywords, the second has plenty. Which resume do you think will fair better in the recruitment process?

RESULTS / ACCOMPLISHMENTS

If you have any notable achievements that can be quantified, be sure to mention those too. Here are some notable achievements worth mentioning:

- Increased customer loyalty or satisfaction
- Decreased customer complaints
- Developed an idea that saved time or money, increased productivity, etc.
- Awards won

- Promotions earned

Even those little compliments your supervisor or managers have made informally can add weight to your application and make for a good story to tell during your interview, so try to remember anything that may be relevant.

Did you make a suggestion for improvements that your superior was particularly impressed by? Did you have an idea for a new service that was implemented? All these things matter.

MINIMISE FRAGMENTATION

If you have a fragmented work history, it will give the impression of a job hopper and this is something you will want to avoid.

The good news is there are many things you can do to draw attention away and minimise the impact . So let's take a look at the options.

COMBINE JOBS

Where several similar consecutive jobs appear or were provided by the same agency, you can combine them into one chunk, for example:

2004–2006 // Front Desk Clerk

Aztec Hotel & Spa, Bloomfields Leisure, Trina's Hair & Beauty Salon

2001–2003 Customer service manager

CS Employment Agency

For summer jobs, you can avoid listing listing specific dates by using a range, for example:

Summer 20xx to Spring 20xx.

ELIMINATE POSITIONS

There are times when it is beneficial to simply drop a position from your résumé. Take a look at the chart below to determine if this could be right for you.

FILL THE GAPS

If you have gaps in your career progression, but were doing something notable during that time, paid or unpaid, you could insert this into the gap to eliminate any unnecessary questions or concern. For instance:

2004–2006 // Fitness Instructor Bloomfields Leisure

2006-2007 // Traveled around Europe or Study Break

2007–2012 // Personal Trainer Wilson Gym

When filling the gaps, observe caution about revealing too much about your personal circumstances. Revealing that you had taken maternity leave will highlight your parental status. Although this may seem harmless, it's not something to advertise when seeking employment.

QUICK TIP

Employment history is a broad term that can include relevant internships, summer or seasonal jobs, part time work, and voluntary placements. Even helping your pops with his self employment business or babysitting can be included if you are struggling to provide relevant experience.

If you have major gaps to fill, take a look at what you were doing during those gaps and see if you can transfer and relate that across.

Other relevant experience (Optional)

Employment history is a broad term that can include relevant internships, summer or seasonal jobs, part time work, and voluntary placements. This is especially important if you have little paid experience.

Education summary

Starting with the most recent and working backwards, include the schools/colleges/universities you have attended. Within each entry, include the year of completion ("In progress" or "expected" are acceptable, if necessary) and award(s) you achieved.

Certifications (Optional)

If you have attended any formal certification courses, e.g., First aid, life saving, then list the details here noting the institution name, date and certification awarded.

Activities & Interests (Optional)

Recreational interests reveal a great deal about your personality and create depth to your character. They also serve as excellent sources of additional skills and experiences, which can be advantageous if you lack certain skills and/or experience.

Generalised list statements such as: 'reading, watching television, sport and socialising' should be avoided, as should unprofessional statements such as: 'I enjoy spending time with my mates, hitting the town and going out on the razz".

Here is an example:

'I have been keen on netball for as long as I can remember and am an active member of my local netball club where I have been captain of the team for 3 years. I have an active interest in nature, and regularly get involved with and manage conservation assignments. To relax, I attend yoga and meditation classes, which help to keep me focused and relieve any build-up of stress.'

This statement gives an immediate impression of someone who is balanced and committed. Their interests highlight several admirable qualities such as team spirit and leadership, and it also details their methods of stress management. A recruitment office would form a positive impression of the candidate based on a statement such as this.

Be mindful about over-indulging in your leisure interests, as the recruiter may get the impression that your hobbies will take priority over your work.

Languages (Optional)

If you have more than one language ability, indicate whether you speak, read, and/or write the language, and include the level to which you are proficient, such as: native, fluent, proficient or basic conversational ability.

References (Optional)

Unless specifically requested, the inclusion of reference information is completely optional.

When listing your references, be sure to include: Name, title, professional relationship to you (e.g. Supervisor, manager and team leader) telephone number and mailing address.

If you decide not to include details, a simple statement such as "References are available on request" is sufficient.

Common mistakes to avoid
Making it all about you

I have always loved to travel and am looking to join a prestigious airline that has lots of amazing destinations and where I can get cheap flights while meeting handsome wealthy men in first class.....

Okay, I am laying that one on thick, but you see my point. The objective is not about you or your needs, it is about what you bring to the airline.

Being vague

Looking for a job as cabin crew with an airline where I can apply my extensive skills and experience.

Hmm, that's not very enticing is it?

Would you want to go through the time and expense of bringing this person to interview when they have some undefined skills and experience, and who seems to not care which airline they work for?

No, and neither does the airline.

Offering no value

I have extensive skills in marketing and development...

STOP!!! Back up a bit.

How is this relevant to a cabin crew position? That's right, it isn't. Next...

If you do come from a background that seems unrelateable, such as marketing and development, dig deeper. Instead of marketing, the ability to influence could be used, and, instead of development, the ability to manage a team.

Now those would be kick ass skills to include.

Zzz

My name is Jane Doe and I come from London, England. I have been working in finance, but I want to make a move to working as cabin crew. I have lots of skills, such as team-working, customer service, and leadership. I also worked within......... and on, on on, and on......

Just remember that this is a brief statement, not an essay. zzzzz sorry, dozed off there for a second. What were we talking about?

You get my point. Keep it short and snappy.

Produce Polished Photographs

A tool for hiring decisions

The requisition of photographs is so much more than a simple vanity requirement, and I cannot emphasise their importance enough. Not only will they serve as a visual reminder for the recruiters to refer back to throughout the assessment process, but they are also used to make hiring decisions long after the interview is over. Airlines place a great deal of value on the photographs, and some will even have very strict requirements about their presentation. For this reason, it is important that you use the following guidelines to create the very best lasting impression.

Strict requirements

Each airline will have its own specific requirements, and these will be advised when you apply. As a general rule, a head and shoulder shot, generally in the form of a 45 x 35 mm passport photograph, and a full-length shot can be expected.

Both are subject to varying specifications and it is vital that you observe those to the letter. I am not kidding. There are some airlines who will not accept your application if the photos do not meet the requirements stated.

Formal vs Casual

Casual shots, while acceptable for some airlines, carry the risk of appearing sloppy, unprofessional, and inappropriate. As a result, they present a much higher risk of rejection. Business attire will give the appearance of professionalism, and are often the minimum acceptable standard if you want to be taken seriously.

Set the scene

A solid backdrop will produce a clean and uncluttered appearance. If possible, use a contrasting colour to avoid blending into the surroundings. And do not under any circumstances use a bed sheet for the backdrop. I've seen it many times and it looks very messy and unprofessional.

Grooming

Photographs tend to exaggerate complexion issues and flatten your features. Use cosmetics to enhance your cheeks, lips and eyes, and apply concealer to diminish spots and blemishes.

Contouring and highlight is a technique that can be used to create depth, balance your face shape, play down flaws, and emphasise assets. Contouring uses a dark shade and is used to recede areas, while highlighting uses a light shade and is used to protrude areas. Try it out and see what a difference it makes to your look.

If you suffer from redness, the camera will pick it up and emphasise it further, so apply some green corrective concealer underneath your foundation to conceal it. Use these with caution as they are very heavy duty and can make you look very pale if over applied.

It is important to control the shine, particularly around the t-zone area, as it will reflect strongly in photos. For minor shine issues, a powder foundation should do the trick. For more problematic skin, an oil absorbing moisturiser or oil balancing gel may be more suitable.

Use eye drops to make your eyes glisten and clear any redness. And for wide awake eyes, try directing your gaze slightly above the camera.

Be sure your hair is neat and well groomed, as frizzy hair or loose ends can be exaggerated in pictures.

For an instant chin tuck, have the photographer position the camera at or just above eye level for the most flattering facial shot.

Summon a warm smile

A warm and sincere smile will complete the look, but creating a beautiful smile on demand is a learned skill, which needs to be practiced.

The fake smile, aptly named the 'Pan-Am Smile' because of the flight attendants of Pan-American Airlines, is simply a courtesy smile that will not translate well in your photos. A 'Duchenne Smile', on the other hand, will provide the most beautiful and sincere looking smile, and this is the smile we are looking to achieve.

Here are some tips that will assist you in generating your photo perfect smile.

Produce a natural smile

The most beautiful smiles are the ones that are natural. If you are using a professional photographer, they will be skilled at drawing out your natural smile, but if you are using an unskilled family member, you will need to channel some of your inner happiness. This can be achieved by thinking of a genuine reason to smile, such as recalling a happy memory, looking at a silly picture, or remembering a good joke.

Fake it till you make it

When it is simply impossible to summons a genuine smile, you will need to fake it. Here are some guidelines that will help.

Time it right:

The secret to producing a relaxed and natural smile is to time it so that you don't have to hold it for too long. Try looking away from the camera, then just before the photograph is taken, face the camera and smile.

Use your eyes:

Smiling eyes are required to complete the look. To achieve this effect, imagine the camera is someone you really fancy. Raise your eyebrows and cheekbones a little, and slightly squint the corners of your eyes. Notice the amazing transformation this creates.

Power Up Your Portfolio

Boost your experience

Experience within a customer-facing role is vital, so if this aspect of your application is shallow or weak, you should certainly consider taking on some additional short-term volunteer or evening work to compensate and strengthen your candidacy. Taking on additional work will show initiative and demonstrate a willingness to work and improve.

Take on volunteer work

Volunteering is beneficial to your application in so many ways. Firstly, it will demonstrate a compassionate and caring side to your personality. Secondly, it will enable you to gain experience and flesh out your skill-set. And third, it will show that you are not motivated by monetary gain.

As a side benefit, you will also gain additional referees who can vouch for you.

Learn new skills

Taking the time to learn new skills will demonstrate your continued dedication to self-improvement and your effort in readying yourself for the position. So consider signing up for mini courses that will be relevant to the position, such as first aid, languages, assertiveness, communication, and leadership. Neither will take much time or money, but the value added to your resume will be substantial.

Engage in extra-curricular activities

Extra-curricular activities can be a hidden gem when it comes to learning new skills and are often under-utilised. If you participate in team sports, it can demonstrate your ability to be a team player. If you coach little league, it will demonstrate your ability to be a leader and if you regularly participate in aerobic activities, it will show that you take pride in your health and fitness. So go out there and have some fun while boosting your candidacy all at the same time.

Mind the gaps

If you are between work when you apply, this can create a damaging gap that will need some explaining or give the wrong impression about your motives. Rather than do nothing during this period of downtime, be proactive by taking on some volunteer work, learning a new skill or sign up for a short course at your local college.

The Group Interview

What to expect

The assessment process varies considerably in length and structure depending on a number of factors. These factors include: The volume of applicants, whether the sessions are held within the airline's premises or a hotel establishment, and whether the sessions are open or invitation only.

Open days typically attract a high volume of candidates and, as such, will often be split over a series of days. Invitation only days, on the other hand, are kept much smaller in number and may span only a few short hours with final interviews conducted on the same day.

In either case, you will be asked to partake is a number of activities. These activities are designed to reveal your personality, competencies and potential for working as cabin crew and are likely to include a series of individual assessments, practical tasks, group discussions and role-play scenarios.

Arrival at the event can seem overwhelming, especially when faced with hundreds of applicants in attendance. You will likely be met with an atmosphere that is friendly and buzzing with adrenaline, but has an eerie sense of tension, as each candidate is anxious to get through the process. This atmosphere generally tapers off as the sessions get underway.

Virgin Atlantic

We began with a brief introduction given by the recruiters, followed by a quick round of mini self presentations about ourselves. The recruiters then handed each of us a card from which to read aloud to the group, this was very short and simple to read. We then carried out a reach test.

Next we were asked to network with the group, taking notes, and then present the information about what I learned about the candidates back to the group. During this task, recruiters picked out candidates for short one on one discussions.

Next we participated in a group discussion. This was based around creating a new advertising campaign for Virgin. We were handed a card with a song written on the back and asked to present our campaign to the tune of that song.

Then the first round of eliminations occurred, with the remaining candidates participating in a series of very simple maths and psychometric tests. Any remaining candidates after this were sent to final interviews.

Emirates

Emirates also began with a brief introduction by the recruiters, alongside a short video presentation. Then the floor opened up to a question and answer session.

At the open day, there was a resume handover, but not at the invitation only day. Several candidates were eliminated after the resume handover, so standing out and focusing on presentation was key when approaching the desk. Reach tests were also carried out at this stage.

After this, we participated in several group discussions, with eliminations taking place between each. We didn't do anything but discussion sessions.

We then filled out some very simple maths, English and aptitude tests and had a mini discussion with the recruiter. Final interviews varied depending on the application method, I done mine at a later date, but many were done the next day.

British Airways

Before anything, British Airways will want to ensure you measure up, so expect to perform a reach test and have your height measured upon arrival. We also had to sit in a jump seat and demonstrate our ability to fasten and unfasten a seatbelt.. Those who failed these tests were sent home.

Next the recruiters gave a short introduction about the airline, and then we were asked to participate in a multiple choice question paper. These are all common sense, and very simple to complete.

Then we went through the various stages of the selection process. I had a group task first. then a role play scenario, and then the two on one interview. The role play lasted only a few minutes and was performed with the recruiter. During the final interview. I was also asked to read from a short script.

As you can see, the approaches are quite different for each airline, and those approaches say a lot about what each airline values the most.

For Virgin, it was all about personality. flair and fun. Coincidentally, extroverted candidates faired well for Virgin.

Emirates were very much about communication. Many extroverted types were eliminated early, with the more introverted types being selected.

British Airways were very well rounded in their approach. covering all bases.

While these are just my observations, you can see that a candidate who may be unsuccessful at Virgin, may do very well at Emirates or BA. This is the corporate culture shining through and needs to be observed if you are to be successful and happy with your choice.

Complacency and the waiting game

With large turnouts, the group will often be split into smaller, more manageable sizes, and assessed in rotation. This means that you will likely find yourself waiting around for long periods between sessions. Although you will not be in a formal assessment during these waiting periods, undercover officers are still assessing you and it is important to remain professional and alert.

Too many candidates allow themselves to relax during these periods, and it is when they relax too much that they become complacent. Just take a look around next time you are at an event and you will see candidates slouching in their seat and generally looking very bored. Don't allow this to happen to you. Move around and network with the other candidates. This will show that you are taking the event seriously and are a friendly sort. As a side benefit, this will make time pass quicker and make the day much more enjoyable. And don't worry about what other candidates will think, as oftentimes they will appreciate your efforts to lighten the atmosphere.

Session breaks are a welcome relief from the mental and emotional stress that the day can induce, but these are especially risky times for becoming complacent, as many candidates do not realise that they are still being watched and assessed.

Just a number

Some airlines have negated to assigning candidates with numbers in place of using their names. This system of designation was introduced to streamline the process and to ensure that candidates are regularly shuffled. The idea behind the system is understandable and efficient, however, there is a disadvantage in that it leaves each candidate severely depersonalised. As such, you are no longer Kate, Alexander, Maria or (insert your name here), but instead you are number 284, 879 or 1029.

Such a system makes it all the more essential that you make an effort to stand out and be recognised.

Avoid the traps during the icebreakers

The recruitment personnel will often start the day with a short introductory briefing and a breakdown of the intended days events. This session should last no more than 30 minutes or so, and allows for any remaining candidates to arrive before the event officially gets underway.

The icebreaker session may involve a short presentation about the airline followed by an open discussion session. During this time, candidates are encouraged to pose questions to the personnel about the airline and the position.

This session is an ideal opportunity to get noticed early, but it can also be a breaking point for those who are unprepared.

Many of the more confident candidates make the mistake of getting carried away with their line of questioning in an attempt to stand out. Unfortunately, asking too many questions at this stage will only demonstrate a general lack of respect for others, who also have questions, and is also more likely to be misconstrued as arrogant, rather than confident. One question really is sufficient.

In asking questions, there is also the added risk looking ill prepared if a question appears unnecessary or has already been answered within the airline literature. This will highlight your lack of research and does not create a favourable first impression.

If you do not have a valid and effective question, it is better to just listen and observe. There will be many more opportunities to get noticed.

Stand out

Once the groups have been arranged and applications submitted, the assessment typically gets underway with a short round of introductions.

As well as learning more about you and your background, these self-introductions are an opportunity for the recruiters to assess how well you cope when addressing a group of people and how articulately you are able to communicate your message while under pressure. In their assessment, they will be looking for good delivery and a certain amount of charisma.

To deliver a self-introduction that makes an impact, here are some guidelines for you to consider.

Make it relevant

Use this opportunity to highlight your suitability for the job of cabin crew by sharing interesting facts about your present or most recent job, and your motives for making a career change.

Be spontaneous

A self-presentation which is spontaneous, rather than rehearsed, will add life and sincerity to your speech. Sure you can prepare a rough draft and familiarise yourself with it, but don't try to learn it by heart, as there is a risk of appearing forced, dull and robotic.

Inject personality

Show your passion and enthusiasm by injecting some emotion and personality into your presentation.

Be concise

Unless advised otherwise, keep it relatively short and focused. Thirty to Sixty seconds should be sufficient.

Rotate your focus

To give the impression of confidence and engage your audience, rotate your gaze and make eye contact with various members for three to five seconds each, then be sure to redirect your focus back to the recruiters to finish your presentation.

Beware of how you sound

Varying your tone, pitch, volume and pace will eliminate the risk of appearing monotone and make it enjoyable for others to listen to. If you are nervous, you may be more inclined to rush. It will help if you make a deliberate attempt to slow your pace slightly.

Consider this example

" Hi everyone. My name is Caitlyn and it's really nice to meet you all. I'm 27 years old and live in the bustling city of Bristol. I currently work as a freelance hair consultant, which is a job I really enjoy, but I have always wanted to be cabin crew, which is why I am here today. Outside of work, I enjoy horse riding and am captain of the local netball team"

A process of elimination

The primary objective during the early stages of the screening process is to filter and eliminate unsuitable candidates as quickly as possible. As such, you will experience periodic elimination sessions throughout the course of the day.

The initial eliminations will typically occur shortly after the first group session, but this is by no means absolute, as schedules are changed regularly and without notice. In any case, it is this first elimination that is the largest and it is likely that 80% or more will leave the process at this stage.

Most airlines will at least try to minimise the amount of stress caused by the eliminations, so they will usually be conducted on a group basis. As the day progresses, and the eliminations become fewer in number, individuals may be taken aside. It would be rare for any one applicant to be singled out or alienated in front of the group.

Naturally the elimination sessions are stressful, but if you make it through the first round, you can be sure that you have made a positive impression. Now as you go forward to the next round, take comfort in knowing that it will be much easier to stand out with fewer numbers in the group, so build on the impression that you have already created and give it all you've got. Use the adrenaline from your early success to carry you through.

Hidden meanings

What recruiters look for

This is the one question I am asked, time and time again. So many candidates overanalyse the process, but the answer is actually very simple. So simple in fact that most of you you will already know what I am going to say.

The recruiters are assessing six key competencies. These are:

- Communication skills
- Interpersonal ability
- Customer focus
- Team spirit
- Leadership
- Initiative

Where confusion occurs

Group tasks are designed so that assessors can view and assess these core competencies first hand, and how you behave during each task will be taken as a clear indication of how you may perform in reality. While it goes without saying that how you behave during an interview is not going to be an accurate representation when compared with a real life scenario, it is through your involvement and behaviour, that assessors can identify positive and negative attributes first hand and be able to make better elimination decisions.

Where most individuals often become confused is between the relevancy of the task and what is actually being observed. Because some of the tasks bear no obvious relevance to the cabin crew role, it is easy to overlook the underlying motives and get caught up in the practicalities of the task instead. And herein lies the trick: The outcome of the task itself is irrelevant.

Focusing on the wrong element

During this segment, most candidates are so intently focused on completing the task correctly and on time that they forget to think about their performance. In most cases, the outcome of the task is actually irrelevant. Assessors are more concerned with how well you perform under pressure and in a team environment, how you communicate your ideas, how you interact with others and what role you assume.

When you think back to the group tasks you have participated in, do you notice that they appear to have no right or wrong answer?

As an example, consider the following group topic:

Topic:

The plane has gone down over the Atlantic Ocean. There are eight survivors, but the one surviving life raft only has a capacity for four people. As a **team**, identify four survivors from the following list who you would save and state your reasons why. Select a spokes-person to **present** your decision and explain why you came up with the answer.

You (the flight attendant) The pope

An ex army general   A surgeon

A pregnant lady   A child

An word class athlete   A nurse

Clearly there is no right answer to this topic, as you wouldn't want to decide such a fate for four people. So what is the point of this task? Take another look at the topic and notice the words I have emphasised are 'team' and 'present'. These are the keys to this task. Assessors are looking to observe how you interact as part of a team, and whether you demonstrate initiative and leadership by volunteering to present the information back to the rest of the group. Most candidates will focus on everything except for those two key points.

Let's take a look at another example: Singing.

Many candidates understand the concept of a discussion or role-play scenario, but just do not understand how singing bears any relevance. Again, this is very simple to comprehend if you read between the lines.

Task:

Many passengers ignore safety demonstrations because they feel they have heard it all before. In an effort to increase safety, Fly High Airlines is considering an overhaul of its safety procedures. As a **team**, come up with a new safety demonstration, which will encourage passengers to pay attention to these important briefings.

The demonstration can include appropriate humour, and must be sung according to the melody given to you on the back of the card. The outcome should be no more than **five minutes** in length and **each individual must participate.**

Seven virtues
Have fun

However silly or irrelevant the tasks may seem, your active involvement is essential. So, rather than concern yourself about external details, just relax and allow yourself to enjoy the process. This positive viewpoint will reflect well on your character, demonstrate enthusiasm, and make the experience a fun filled one for you.

Contribute

Contributing ideas and making suggestions is another great way to demonstrate your enthusiasm and team spirit. It will show that you are able to express yourself and are keen to get involved.

Volunteer

There are times when no candidate wants to put their neck on the line, so volunteering is a great way to demonstrate your enthusiasm and it will show that you are not afraid to take the initiative.

Summarise

Summarising the main points of a discussion is a great way to move past awkward moments of silence and sticking points. The breathing room summarising creates will typically stimulate further ideas and encourage participation. Not only will your peers be grateful for the momentary relief, your communication and leadership ability will also be highlighted.

Use names

Remembering people's names will demonstrate your ability to listen and pay attention to detail. Moreover, it will demonstrate a tremendous amount of respect for others and create a lasting impact.

Be positive

When you choose to exhibit a positive spirit, people will naturally be drawn towards your character. So, be enthusiastic about the exercises you are asked to undertake and be encouraging towards others.

Encourage

If any members of your team remain reserved, encourage their involvement by asking if they have an idea, suggestion or opinion. This shows empathy, consideration and team spirit.

Deadly sins
Over involvement

Getting involved and showing enthusiasm in a task is fantastic, but over involvement and incessant talking can leave others struggling to get involved and may transfer across to assessors as arrogance. Always provide others with an opportunity to provide their opinion.

Under involvement

For assessors to make an informed assessment, active involvement from each individual is essential. Those who are unable to get involved, for whatever reason, will surely be eliminated.

Disputing

Conflicting views are natural, however, a group assessment is neither the time or place to engage in a hostile dispute with other candidates.

Criticising

Even if your intentions are honourable and the feedback is constructive, criticising another candidates opinions, actions and ideas may be perceived as an attack. An assessment day is neither the time nor the place.

Being negative

Making negative remarks or exhibiting frustration over tasks, peers or previous employers , no matter how harmless it may seem, will raise serious concerns about your attitude and ethics.

Being bossy

There is nothing wrong with striving for excellence, however, being dominant and imposing your ideas on others is overbearing and intimidating. This always leads others to feel incompetent.

Not listening

Neglecting to listen to instructions leads to misinterpretations and displays a general lack of enthusiasm. Not listening or talking over others is ignorant and disrespectful.

Active involvement is essential...

I know it goes without saying, and I've covered this briefly above, but it bears repeating that it is only through your active involvement that recruiters are able to assess your suitability and identify your positive attributes. So however silly or irrelevant the tasks may seem, or how difficult it is to get your opinion across, your involvement is essential.

Rather than concern yourself about external details, just relax and allow yourself to enjoy the process. This positive viewpoint will reflect well on your character, demonstrate enthusiasm, and make the experience a fun filled one for you.

I understand that it can be difficult to get involved when you are in a group of individuals who have big personalities. They set off on a tangent, leaving you feeling like you are on the outside struggling to get in. While these conditions do pose a difficult challenge, it is absolutely essential that you do what you can to be included. Raise your hand if you need to, but whatever you do, don't remain on the outside.

If you suffer from nervousness, understand that it is okay to be nervous, even permissible, but allowing your nerves to keep you from getting involved is not. It is better to risk displaying your nerves than it is to remain silent. At least the recruiters will appreciate your effort. If your nerves are strong to the point that you become debilitated, turn back to part 3 for in-depth guidance, tips and tricks.

... But don't overdo it

Getting involved and showing enthusiasm in a task is fantastic, but over involvement and incessant talking can leave others struggling to get involved and may transfer across to assessors as arrogance.

If you do notice that other members of your team remain reserved or appear to be struggling to get involved, encourage their involvement by asking if they have an idea, suggestion or opinion. This is a clear indication of empathy, consideration and team spirit and it is these qualities that recruiters will be impressed by.

Your scorecard

To make an effective evaluation, the recruiters will typically refer to a competency rating scale. This scale works on a points based system and the final result will reflect a candidate's suitability for the position.

	-1 Unacceptable	0 Needs Improvement	1 Effective	2 Proficient	3 Outstanding

3	Works effectively as a team member and builds strong relationships within it
0	Remains calm and confident, and responds logically and decisively in difficult situations
3	Understands other people's views and takes them into account
2	Contributes ideas and collaborates with the team
0	Takes a systematic approach to problem solving
3	Speaks with authority and confidence
3	Is thoughtful and tactful when dealing with people
-1	Is conscientious of completing tasks on time
3	Actively supports and encourages others
-1	Participates as an active and contributing member of the team

Group Tasks

Practical Tasks

Bridging the Gap

Instructions

With the materials provided, design and construct a bridge which strong enough to support a roll of sticky tape.

Materials

- » 5 sheets of A4 paper
- » A pair of scissors
- » 1 Metre length of sticky tape
- » 4 Drinking straws
- » 1 Metre length of string
- » 2 Elastic bands

Let Me Entertain You

Duration: 40 Minutes

Instructions

As you reach cruising altitude, you discover that the in flight entertainment system has failed.

To ensure the passengers are entertained for the duration of the four hour flight, design a game concept and <u>present</u> it to the rest of the group in a teaching style.

Advertising Space

Instructions

Fly High Airlines has secured a prime time radio spot and needs a new commercial campaign.

Using the team's collective <u>knowledge of the airline</u>, create a compelling commercial that will attract new customers.

The final broadcast must be no more than <u>45 seconds</u> in length, and <u>each team member must have an active role</u> in the final presentation.

Points to Consider

This activity will highlight your knowledge of the airline, so be ready with plenty of input from your research.

Designer Wear

Duration: 45 Minutes

Instructions

Fly High Airlines is looking to update its image and needs new designs for its cabin crew uniform.

Consider the existing design and come up with a new or modified concept.

Points to Consider

During this task, be mindful of what is considered appropriate to the culture.

Also, take inspiration from the current design as it provides valuable insight into what the airline considers to be appropriate.

Group discussions

Instructions

Your flight is scheduled to land in Los Angeles, however, due to mechanical difficulties the plane was forced to land on a remote island.

During landing, much of the equipment aboard was damaged, but 10 items have been recovered intact. Your task is to rank them in terms of their importance for your crew.

Items

- » A box of matches
- » 15 feet of nylon rope
- » 5 gallons of water
- » Signal flares
- » A self inflating life raft

- » A magnetic compass
- » First aid kit
- » A fruit basket
- » A tub of dry milk powder
- » A shotgun

Day Trip

Instructions

You have been given the responsibility for arranging a day trip for 15 disabled children. Discuss where you would take the children, what activities you would have arranged and why.

Options

- » Theme park
- » Museum
- » White water rafting
- » Trip on the Orient Express
- » Water Park
- » Safari
- » Art gallery
- » Scenic helicopter ride

Points to Consider

In this instance, the children in question are disabled. So, certain activities will not be appropriate, while others may not sufficiently capture the children's interest. It is important to gain a balance between having fun and being safe.

Role Play Scenarios

Role-play scenarios may be performed with other candidates as a pair or within a group, or they may be performed one on one with an assessor.

The scenarios will bear some relation to the demands of the job and are likely to include:

Intoxicated passenger   Disorderly behaviour

Terrorist threat   Disruptive child

Toilet smoker   Abusive behaviour

Fearful passenger   Passenger complaint

The assessors don't expect you to know the answer to every possible scenario they introduce. They simply want to see how you react in challenging situations. So, when taking part in any role play scenario, use the following guidelines:

- Be proactive and do your best to resolve the situation using your initiative
- Remain calm and composed
- Be direct and assertive
- Immerse yourself into the role
- Take each scenario seriously
- Devise a plan and follow it as much as possible

Here are some pointers to help you deal with some common scenarios:

Complaint

In the case of a passenger complaint, it is important that you listen to their concern without interruption. Ask questions, where appropriate, to clarify their concerns and show empathy towards their situation. If the facts warrant it, apologise for the situation, explain what action you intend to take and thank them for bringing the matter to your attention.

Fearful passenger

If a passenger is fearful of flying, be considerate of their feelings. Use a gentle and calm tone to talk them through the flight and reassure them of any sounds or sensations they may experience. Let the passenger know where you can be found and show them the call bell.

Intoxicated passenger

Offer the passenger a cup of tea or coffee and don't provide any more alcoholic drinks. You could also encourage the passenger to eat some food. Remain calm towards the passenger, but be direct and assertive in your approach. If you feel it appropriate, inform your senior and seek assistance from other crew-members.

The Final Interview

What to expect

Congratulations if you have made it through to the final interview. Having assessed your involvement and performance during the group sessions, the recruiters have clearly observed qualities in your character that they admire, and would now like to explore your motives further. So revel in the success you have achieved to this point, and be ready to close out this process.

During the final interview, the recruiters will seek to explore your motives for applying to the airline and your desire for pursuing a career as cabin crew. Moreover, they will seek to gather information about your work history, character and work ethic to determine whether you will fit the job and airline.

To ease you into the interview process, and make you feel more relaxed, the recruiters will typically open the session with questions about you and your background. They will then seek to explore your motivation for applying to the airline and making a career change. Questions such as "Why do you want to work for us?" and "Why do you want to be cabin crew?" are common at this stage.

With the interview thoroughly under way, the recruiters will want to determine whether you possess the skills and experience necessary for the position. Here you can expect more probing situational and behavioural questions, such as "When have you handled a customer complaint?" and "Describe a time when you failed to communicate effectively".

Although there appears to be no typical duration for panel interviews, you can expect a baseline time of at least 20 minutes, to upwards of 1 hour or more. In either case, the duration has no bearing on your ultimate success; so do not overly concern yourself with this aspect. An interview lasting just 20 minutes doesn't indicate a failure, just as an interview in excess of 1 hour does not indicate success.

Ice-breaker or deal-breaker

The interviewers will have several tricks up their sleeves to extract information during the course of the interview, but it is during the pre-interview 'ice breaking' session that you must be extra cautious.

During the first few moments of an interview it is only natural that most candidates will be feeing nervous, and it is under the rush of adrenaline that candidates are most likely to reveal too much information. It is also during these first few moments that candidates get caught off guard because they expect to be softly broken into the interview before the interrogation actually begins. Interviewers use this assumption to their advantage.

Personnel are trained to use trick questions, in the form of icebreakers, to get candidates to inadvertently volunteer sensitive and personal information about their circumstances and background. They will use friendly manipulation and small talk to lull candidates into a false sense of security. Under these conditions, they are able to extract information very easily from unsuspecting candidates.

So, whatever happens and however relaxed the interviewers attempt to make you feel, remember that you are being assessed and you need to keep your whit's about you.

Meet the recruitment team

Typically, there will be two or three official recruitment officers present during the final interview. These officers may be HR personnel, or they may be working senior crew-members. Either way, you can be sure that they are experienced recruitment professionals.

To successfully interact with these recruitment personnel, it is important to understand their styles and be prepared to deal with them accordingly. Within a cabin crew interview setting, you will typically encounter two dominant styles of interviewer. I call these: The interrogation experts and the guardian angels.

The interrogation expert

Interrogation experts believe that candidates will only show their true personalities while under intense pressure. As a result, they adopt a direct and intimidating style of questioning and will cross-examine every answer you provide. During this onslaught of questioning, they will be observing your ability to remain calm and think on your feet. So, approach their questions in a calm and confident manner and be direct and succinct in your response.

The guardian angel

Guardian angels will attempt to relieve the pressure of the atmosphere by engaging in friendly conversation. While their relaxed and friendly style can be a welcome relief, unsuspecting candidates may become overly casual and reveal more than is appropriate. Caution is therefore advised to avoid being culled by these friendly tactics. You certainly don't to want to appear rigid, but you do need to be mindful of who you are talking to and remain professional.

What assessors really look for

Recruiters understand that you will not be able to answer every question perfectly, and they also understand that you may not know the answer to each question that is asked. What they do expect and what they are invested in is how you respond to certain lines of questioning and how you conduct yourself. As such, their line of questioning will be designed to reveal your ability to:

- Listen actively
- Express yourself articulately, confidently and professionally
- Answer questions logically and concisely
- Remain calm under pressure

Some of the questions are designed specifically to throw you off guard, to see how you react to the pressure. With these sorts of questions, the interviewers are not necessarily looking for a perfect answer, but they are looking for a quick and well-prepared response.

They will also use several tactics to elicit a negative reaction or encourage you to reveal more than you should. This may be through the use of the silent treatment (as discussed in part 1), or through a line of questioning that is designed to keep you from knowing the correct answer. They will use trick questions, behavioural questions and even trick questions in the guise of a positive question, all in an attempt to rattle you and make you fall apart during the process.

Ultimately, it is important to remember that the recruiters are looking to hire positive people, so it is important to remain calm and composed throughout the interview and never show that you have been flustered.

Seven deadly sins
Controlling

Trying to lead or control the conversation will appear arrogant and disrespectful. Ask questions when appropriate opportunities arise, but allow the recruiter to do his or her job.

Interrupting

Interruptions are rude and disrespectful to the speaker. So, unless absolutely necessary, you should allow the recruiter to finish speaking before responding or asking for clarification.

Lying

If you lie, there will be a very good chance that you will be caught out when the recruiters probe into your answers with follow up questions. If this happens, you could end up looking rather silly and, worse still, any chance of being offered the job will be ruined.

Talking incessantly

It's easy to talk too much when nervous, however, it is important to remember that interviews are two-way exchanges. A moment of silence, while it might seem awkward to you, lets the recruiter know that you are done and allows them to move the interview along.

Being negative

Making negative remarks or exhibiting frustration over tasks, peers, other airlines or previous employers, no matter how harmless it may seem, will raise serious concerns about your attitude and ethics.

Overusing filler words

The useless and annoying verbal mannerisms "you know," "like," "in other words," "kind of," "ummm," and "anyways." should be avoided at all costs. Besides making you sound unprofessional, they also detract attention from your message.

Unprepared and unnecessary questions

To stand out as an informed and competent applicant, your questions should reflect that you have researched the airline and the position. Asking questions that have already been addressed within the airline's literature will make you appear unprepared and incompetent. Likewise, asking questions that are based on money and benefits will make you appear selfishly motivated and give a negative impression about your motives for the position and/or the airline.

Avoid robotic, flat, and boring answers

In preparing for the final interview, it may make sense to memorise some of your answers. Unfortunately, trying to memorise an answer for every scenario will only work against you. Not only do you run the risk of sounding like a robot, with a boring and flat delivery, but you also risk forgetting your answers and appearing flustered as you try to recall the information.

Rather than memorising your answers, make a list of key points and try to remember those instead. Key points are much easier to remember than lengthy sentences and will allow you to create a genuine and spontaneous answer based around that point.

Another technique, that is highly effective and advantageous, is to prepare through actual practice. Whether that is through a role play with a friend or family member, the use of a camcorder or through attending mock interviews with other airlines, practice will allow you to feel much more confident and natural when you do the real thing.

Demonstrate respect for the recruiter

It is important to be observant and sense when the interviewer has heard enough about a particular point. Many candidates go off on a tangent when they get into the swing of the interview, and neglect to notice that the interviewer wants to move on. To demonstrate your respect for the recruiter and his or her time, you could ask "Would you like me to elaborate on that further?" The interviewer will appreciate your effort.

Eek, I don't know the answer

You are not expected to know the answer to every question you are asked. In fact, the interviewer may throw you a curve ball on purpose in order to test you reaction and observe how you respond under the pressure.

Bluffing your way through an answer, for the sake of not wanting to admit that you don't know the answer, will not reflect favourably on you. The interviewer will be much more forgiving if you are honest and admit your lack of knowledge on a particular point.

If you lack relative experience in a particular area, you may consider elaborating on a similar and alternative aspect, or you can take the opportunity to remind them of the skills that you do have and explain how you would tackle the situation if it arose. For instance: "I can't remember ever being in that situation, however, I did face something slightly similar that I could tell you about?".

Run of the mill clichés wil not cut it

Answers such as "I'm a workaholic" or "I'm a perfectionist" or "I try too hard to please everyone" are tired old cliché's and are simply not going to cut it. While they may be true statements, recruiters are not naive and they certainly will not accept generic responses such as these.

Generic answers will only make you sound just like everyone else and will not do you any favours. You need to be more creative and, more importantly, you need to sound sincere.

Stand out as an informed candidate

Taking the time to research an airline you want to work for will enable you to ask intelligent questions, as well as answer any that are posed. Your informed knowledge will give a positive impression about you and your motivation to work for the airline, thus giving you a competitive edge over less informed candidates.

If you know nothing about the airline other than the colour of the uniform, the salary and their best destinations, you certainly won't create a positive impression.

There is no need to know the whole history of the airline, but you should at least know some basic information, such as:

- What is their route network?
- Are there any future plans for expansion or growth?
- Where is their base airport located?
- Who are the airline's major competitors?
- What do you like about this particular airline?
- How long have they been operating?
- Has the airline won any awards? If so, which ones?

Winning formula
Answers as easy as ABC

When preparing your answers to traditional questions, keep the A.B.C formula in mind.

A: Answer

Make your answer concise by answering the question directly

B: Back it up

Back up your answer with solid facts. This will add a lot of weight to any statements made.

C: Conclude

The conclusion allows you to expand on your skills and what you can offer the airline

Consider the following example:

What is your best attribute?

Answer:

"As you will have observed during the group assessments, I am a very welcoming and social individual who interacts well with others, and readily adapts to new people and environments."

Back it up:

"In fact, my previous supervisor also picked up on these attributes and often asked me to carry out the client shampoo because she knew I would make the clients feel welcome and relaxed"

Conclude:

"I am confident that this aspect of my character will enable me to perform the job to the same high standard that exists currently within the airline"

ACT on negative questions

Negative questions can be better approached using the A.C.T formula.

A: Attack

By attacking the question head on, not only do you avoid being alienated by the question, it also allows you to swiftly move on and add clarity to your response.

C: Clarify

This is your opportunity to add any clarity and facts that may support or justify your answer.

T: Turn

Now turn the focus away from the initial negative question to focus on the positive outcome of the experience.

Consider the following example:

What is your greatest weakness?

Attack:

"I recognise that my leadership ability is a potential area of improvement"

Clarify:

"Which is why I am actively working on developing this area further through a part time training course at my local college"

Turn:

"Although I am still learning, I see constant improvement in my capabilities when being faced with leadership tasks and I am confident that I will continue to learn and grow with experience"

Winning answers with the SARR formula

When preparing your examples to competency-based questions, the S.A.R.R formula can help you structure your response.

S: Situation

Briefly describe the challenge, problem, or task

A: Action

Describe what you did and how you did it

R: Result

Describe the outcome and how your actions affected the outcome or the people involved

R: Reflection

Elaborate on what you learned from the experience and whether you would do things differently in the future.

Consider the following example:

When have you used your initiative to solve a problem?

Situation:

"I was in the staff room during my lunch break, and I could hear a lot of noise coming from inside the salon. I went to investigate and two, very bored, little girls confronted me. I could sense that their excitement was causing a disruption and inconvenience"

Action:

"I immediately took the initiative and attempted to occupy them by offering to plait their hair while they made bracelets from some hair beads. Their eyes sparkled with excitement and I was able to keep them occupied for the remainder of their visit"

Result:

"We had lots of fun and, while the calm was restored, the stylist was able to complete the clients' treatment"

Reflection:

"I felt really pleased that with just a little extra effort, I had made such a big difference"

Probing with follow-up questions

Follow up questions are either used to verity the viability of your answer, or to tempt negative information into the open. So it is important to have examples ready to back up any statements made.

Prepare to be asked:

- What did you learn from the experience?
- What specifically did you say?
- How did you feel?
- Would you do anything differently?
- How did they react?
- What other options did you consider?
- Why did you decide to take the action that you did?
- You mentioned ... Tell me more about that.
- How did you retain your composure?

- Can you give me an example of that?
- Can you be more specific about...?

The constant interruption

In an attempt to throw you off, the recruiter may even interrupt your responses with supplementary probing questions.

Take a look at the following example.

When have you disagreed with a colleague?

Candidate

"Working in a creative environment with other highly skilled professionals, it was natural that we had the occasional clash of ideas."

Recruiter

"Please can you elaborate further?"

Candidate

"We would sometimes have a clash of ideas based around our individual preference towards certain products, styles, magazines or equipment. Although, any disagreements we did have were relatively minor and insignificant."

Recruiter

"What would you consider minor and insignificant?"

Candidate

"Our debates were never confrontational, and they never interfered with our work in any way. In fact, some disagreements were quite educational."

Recruiter

"Educational?"

Candidate

"Yes, some very interesting views emerged from these debates which sometimes resulted in people, including myself, having a slight change in perspective."

Recruiter

"Can you tell me about a change you had in perspective following such a debate?"

It is important to answer the questions without demonstrating any frustration or resentment, Once you have answered the question, smile and get straight back on point.

Frequent Questions

Tell me about yourself

This question is usually asked early as an ice breaker. There is no need to delve into your childhood leisure pursuits here, the recruiters simply want a paraphrased overview of what you do, why you are attending the interview and what you have to offer.

"As you can see from my résumé, I currently work as a freelance hair consultant, and have worked in client-facing roles for the past eight years. During this time, I have worked my way up from a receptionist to a senior hair stylist, while simultaneously studying for my NVQ levels 1, 2 and 3.

Now, this brings me to why I am here today, interviewing with you.

I have always wanted to become cabin crew and, during the course of my career, I have been gradually mastering the skills needed to perform its tasks. I'm confident that the customer care and teamwork skills I have developed throughout the course of my career, combined with my friendly and positive nature, will complement your existing team and enable me to deliver the standard of service that passengers have come to expect from Fly High Airlines.

I'd now like to discuss how I might continue my success by joining your team."

Why do you want to become cabin crew?

An honest and passionate response to this question will surely set you apart. Think about it, why do you really want the job? Where did the desire come from? Was it a childhood dream, or was it sparked by another interest?

"As a child, I was fascinated by aircraft and always felt a buzz of excitement when planes flew overhead.

This is where my passion for flying initially began, but it wasn't until I carried out a career suitability test at college that I really started to consider cabin crew as a serious future prospect.

The test examined personal attributes, interests and skills, and the final result came back suggesting suitability for the occupation.

I done some further research into the job and instantly agreed. This job is tailored to my personality, skills and experience and is one I will feel committed to. Moreover, it is one I am confident that I will be good at."

Why should we hire you?

This is the time to shine, so don't be modest. Consider the experience and character traits that are most relevant and transferable to the position and explain how you have demonstrated these in the past.

Answer

"As you can see from my résumé, I have worked in client facing roles for the past eight years. So, I am certainly qualified to perform the diverse requirements of this role. Also, the fact that I have been promoted through the ranks is a clear testament to my abilities and the confidence my manager had in me.

Back It Up

More significantly, my character is tailored to the role. As you will have observed during the group assessments, I am a very welcoming and social individual who interacts well with others. I readily adapt to new people and environments, I am hard working and think fast on my feet.

Conclude

I am confident that these aspects of my personality and experience will enable me to perform the job to the same high standard that exists currently."

Why do you want to work for us?

To make the greatest impact, begin with a personal story, but close with a demonstration of your knowledge and fit for the airline. This will make you stand out as an informed and enthusiastic individual who has something more to offer.

"My first passenger experience with Fly High Airlines was two years ago, on a flight from Dubai to Los Angeles. The service on board was so immaculate and welcoming, that I was instantly impressed. Following this experience I became a frequent flyer and, when I decided to apply for this position, I was in no doubt who I want to work for.

Once I started to research the airline further, I was pleased to discover that the airlines corporate culture holds true with my own values and beliefs. Specifically the open door policy and customer comfort initiatives. This discovery reinforced my desire further and confirmed my belief that I will indeed complement your existing team."

What are your best qualities?

Don't be shy, give it all you got. But, be sure to back it up with examples.

Answer

"As you will have observed during the group assessments, I am a very welcoming and social individual who interacts well with others, and readily adapts to new people and environments."

Back it up

"In fact, my previous supervisor also picked up on these attributes and often asked me to carry out the shampoo because she knew I would make the clients feel welcome and relaxed"

Conclude

"I am confident that these aspects of my character will enable me to perform the job to the same high standard that exists currently within the airline"

What is your greatest weakness?

The key to answering questions about weaknesses is to focus your response on those skills you are actively learning or planning to develop. This could be assertiveness or leadership. The point is, it is only a weakness because you haven't yet mastered it, and that is why you are working on developing those skills further.

Attack:

"I recognise that my leadership ability is a potential area of improvement"

Clarify:

"Which is why I am actively working on developing this area further through a part time training course at my local college"

Turn:

"Although I am still learning, I see constant improvement in my capabilities when being faced with leadership tasks and I am confident that I will continue to learn and grow with experience"

What qualities are necessary for cabin crew?

The recruiters want to know that you understand what the role involves and what qualities are necessary to perform its tasks. Conclude this answer by acknowledging your skills in relation to the position.

"Cabin crew play a vital role in giving a good impression of the airline as a whole. This means crew members need to have good communication and customer care skills, as well as a friendly and welcoming demeanour.

Because of the importance of safety, it is also important that they have the strength of character to cope with difficult people and situations, in a calm and objective manner.

These are all attributes I possess, and are the primary reasons I would complement your existing team."

Why did you leave your last job?

While you do need to be honest about your reasons for leaving past employment, you need to be diplomatic in your response. Being bored or not getting along with your boss are not ideal answers here.

No opportunities

"While I enjoyed working for my previous employer, and appreciate the skills I developed while I was there, I felt I was not being challenged enough in the job. After working my way up through the company, there were no further opportunities for advancement."

Redundancy

"I survived the first layoffs, but unfortunately this one got me."

Temporary position

"The job was only a temporary position which I took to broaden my experience."

What do you know about our airline?

This is where your research will pay off handsomely. So, demonstrate your enthusiasm by sharing knowledge that will reveal the effort you have taken to learn more about the airline and its operations.

"Fly High Airlines began operating in 1980 with a single leased aircraft, serving just two destinations. The airline now serves 73 destinations in 48 countries worldwide and is rapidly expanding its route network, which is soon to include Bristol and Ohio.

As a testament to the airlines excellent standard of service, it has acquired over 250 international awards for customer service excellence, and is now one of the largest and popular airlines in the world."

What do you dislike about your current job?

There will always be less than exciting aspects of a job, however, being critical about your job isn't going to create a positive impression. So, soften these aspects as much as possible and try to select neutral examples, such as paperwork, lack of job security or opportunities for growth.

"I honestly can't think of any major dislikes. I don't think I'd be able to really excel if I weren't truly interested in the work, or if I were merely motivated by its financial rewards. I guess my answer will have to come under the category or nuisances.

The biggest nuisance is the paperwork. I realise the importance of documentation, and I cooperatively fill out the forms, but I'm always looking for efficiencies in that area that will get me out in front of the client where I belong."

Behavioural Questions

When have you gone out of your way for a customer?

Evaluation

Those candidates who demonstrate that they always put in extra effort to provide a better and more complete service will surely have an advantage.

Your answer should demonstrate that you always go the extra mile, and never deliver a merely acceptable standard.

Sample Response 1

Situation:

I had a client call into the store who was looking for a very specific style of fabric. She had visited several stores in and around the area but hadn't been successful in her search.

I could see that she was exhausted, but also very determined. She spoke with such sorrow in her voice that I actually began to feel sorry for the poor lady because I didn't have the fabric to sell her.

Action:

Not wanting to be the bearer of more bad news, I decided to offer my assistance. I spent several hours ringing around wholesalers, distributors and manufacturers trying to track down this particular fabric, when finally I struck gold with a small manufacturing plant.

Result:

Because the fabric was a special order, there was a small handling charge, but the customer received the fabric within a few days and was sure it was worth the expense and wait.

Sample Response 2

Situation:

I encountered a problem when one of my clients was unable to have a hair treatment carried out in her home because it was being renovated.

Action:

In an attempt to keep the client, I spoke to a contact I had within a local salon and was able to negotiate a small fee for use of the salon facilities.

Result:

This worked out really well because it was convenient for both myself and the client to travel to. Since then, I have negotiated similar deals with four other salons and have increased my customer base dramatically as a direct result.

Describe a time when your customer service could have been better?

Evaluation

Providing excellent customer service is vital, so you should be very cautious when providing negative examples.

You could take a modest approach and explain that you always strive to do better, or you could be honest with humble example.

Alternatively, you could attempt to avoid providing an example by explaining how you maintain your standards, and then proceed with an example of a time when you have demonstrated this capability.

Sample Response (Modest approach)

I take great pride in providing the best service I possibly can, but in doing so I increase my skills and can always see room for improvement.

Sample Response (No experience)

I take great pride in providing the best service I possibly can, and I never let my standards slip. Even during times of high pressure, I make an effort to remain courteous and helpful. I can honestly say that I have never received any negative feedback.

When have you solved a customer problem?

Evaluation

The recruiter wants to get an idea of how you apply your initiative and problem-solving skills to customer related issues. A good answer here will demonstrate that you always put in extra effort to provide good customer service and are not intimidated by difficult situations.

Sample Response

Situation:

I remember a client who came to me to have her hair extensions replaced. She had worn sewn in extensions for several months and was experiencing some discomfort from the attachments.

Action:

As I examined her hair, I was shocked to discover how much damage had been caused. Her roots had become severely matted and the tightness from the installed tracks had created spots of baldness.

I took a moment to analyse the situation, work out a strategy and then I set to work.

I spent several hours meticulously untangling every hair and removing every extension piece, The more I removed, the more I could see the scale of the damage that had been caused. Sadly, the client's hair was in very bad shape after the removal and the spots of baldness were very evident. Needless to say, I had a very emotional customer.

I applied a very deep conditioning protein treatment to the customers remaining locks and gave it a good trim. I then finished up with some fine and strategically placed fusion hair extensions to conceal the bald patches and create some much needed volume.

Result:
Following the treatment, the client looked fantastic and her smile was restored. Her hair soon returned to its former glory and she became a regular client of mine.

When have you tended to an upset customer?

Evaluation

The recruiter is trying to grasp your ability to cope with stressful situations. A good answer will suggest that you can think on your feet, and display a positive and patient attitude when challenging situations arise.

Sample Response

Situation:

I recently experienced a situation with a client who was having relationship problems. She was becoming increasingly emotional and I could sense that she was feeling very depressed.

Action:

Although I felt compassion for her situation, I knew that it was important for me not to get overly involved. So, I gave her chance to talk while I listened, and I tried to show empathy while remaining neutral and professional in my response.

Result:

Just being able to talk to someone who listened seemed to make her feel better. As she continued to speak, she appeared to have gained a deeper insight into her situation and actually began seeing things more positively. Consequently, she was able to calmly discuss her feelings with her partner and work through their problems. She later thanked me for listening.

Reflection:

From this experience, I learned that just listening can be providing good customer care.

Have you been confronted by an aggressive customer?

Evaluation

The ability to remain well-mannered and well-tempered while dealing with an aggressive customer is an absolute necessity. The recruiter will want to assess whether you can deal with confrontational issues in a calm and rational manner.

You will be assessed on how well you coped under the pressure and how you dealt with the customer. A good response will show that you never lost your temper and remained courteous throughout the experience.

Sample Response

Situation:

Shortly after I began freelancing, I encountered a problem when an associate of mine tried to pressure me into a free service based on friendship.

Action:

I proceeded to offer her, what I considered to be, a reasonable discount, but she was not satisfied with my offer and proceeded to pressure me with emotional blackmail. I remained cordial, but became more assertive as I continued to refuse her demands.

Result:

Rather than accept the reasons for my decision, she became increasingly enraged, and even began to slander my service and friendship

Shocked at her over-reaction, and concerned about what might develop, I felt I had no option but to withdraw from the situation.

Reflection:

This experience was very challenging and certainly tested my patience. But I remained calm and, although this particular relationship never recovered, it was a learning experience that hasn't since been repeated.

When have you had to say 'No' to a customer?

Evaluation

There will be occasions when it is necessary to say no to a passenger. The recruiter wants to know that you aren't intimidated by such situations and have the strength of character to deal with the situation authoritatively, yet diplomatically.

You will be assessed on how you approached the customer and went about dealing with the situation. A good response will demonstrate your ability to use tact, and will show that you remained courteous throughout the experience.

Sample Response

Situation:

I remember when a customer tried to return a pair of trainers to the store for a refund. Although the customer denied it, I could see that the shoes had clearly been worn.

Action:
I remained calm and polite as I suggested that the shoes could not be returned unless faulty or unused.

The customer become very aggressive and repeatedly threatened to contact our head office to complain about me if I didn't refund him immediately.

I remained assertive and suggested this would be the best course of action for him to take. I then proceeded to provide him with the full details of our complaints manager within the head office.

Result:
Realising defeat, the man stormed out of the shop and, to my knowledge, never did take the matter further.

When have you handled a customer complaint?

Evaluation

The recruiter wants to know that you are able to retain your composure and use your problem solving skills when dealing with a dissatisfied customer.

A good response will show that you never took the complaint personally, remained calm and courteous, and were able to create a satisfactory outcome for the customer.

Sample Response

Situation:

I remember when a customer complained about a meal they had purchased.

Because over two thirds of the entire course had been eaten, not only was it obvious that the complaint was insincere, but it was also against the restaurants policy to offer a refund under such circumstances.

The customer was becoming very enraged and threatened to write to the trading standards and newspapers if I did not give him a full refund.

Action:

I gave the customer my undivided attention while he vented his frustrations. Then, when he had finally calmed down, I calmly apologised for the dissatisfaction and proceeded to offer a meal deal voucher as a goodwill gesture.

Result:

The customer was clearly unhappy not to have received a refund, but he left the restaurant and, as suspected, never did take the matter any further.

When have you had to resolve a conflict between what the customer wanted and what you could realistically deliver?

Evaluation

The recruiter wants to determine that you have the strength of character to voice your concerns. They also want to see that you can be diplomatic, yet authoritative, in your communication style.

You will be assessed on how you approached the customer and how you dealt with the situation.

Sample Response

Situation:

I remember a client who came to me for a colour treatment and restyle. She had used a virtual hairstyle software to create her ideal look and was beaming with excitement as she showed me the picture.

The style was notably very pretty, and it was clear that it was ideally suited to the client. Unfortunately, however, the client's hair had been through several perming and colour treatments, and the platinum blonde shade that she wanted just wasn't going to be possible at that time.

Action:

Knowing how excited the client was, I felt a little dejected as I proceeded to break this news to her.

In the hope of relieving some of her obvious disappointment, I suggested a strand test to see if it would be possible to lift some of the colour without causing excessive damage. If the strand test were a success, we could perform a gradual transformation through the use of highlights.

Result:

Thankfully, the strand test was a success and the client, while naturally disappointed, was happy to go ahead with the gradual transformation. The result was striking,and the client was happy with the result.

Within nine months, the transformation was complete, and I had a very satisfied customer.

Describe a situation when the customer was wrong

Evaluation

Although the popular saying suggests otherwise, the customer isn't always right and the recruiter wants to know that you aren't Intimidated by such situations.

You will be assessed on how you approached the customer and went about dealing the situation. A good response will demonstrate your ability to use tact, and will show that you remained courteous throughout the experience.

Sample Response

Situation:

I remember a client who I had carried out a perming treatment for. After completing the treatment, I provided written instructions for how to care for her new perm which specifically instructed against washing the hair for at least 48 hours.

Unfortunately, the very next day the client washed her hair and the perm dropped out. The client was understandably very upset, but refused to accept that the perm had fallen out as a consequence of her own actions. She became very irate and started to slander my work and the salon.

Action:
When asked if she had followed the instructions, she denied being provided with any. I assured her that instructions were provided, and suggested she check her belongings.

Result:
Later that afternoon, the client returned to the salon holding onto the instruction sheet with a very embarrassed look on her face. She apologised profusely for her behaviour.

Reflection:
To avoid a repeat of this situation, I now provide clearer warnings within the written information sheet and back it up with verbal instructions.

Have you ever bent the rules for a customer?

Evaluation

There are situations where it is permissible to bend the rules, however, some airlines may view rule bending very negatively. So, no matter how trivial or well-intended, you may want to play it safe and declare that you have never gone against the rules.

If you do decide to provide an answer, you should show that you are able to keep balance between company policy and the interest of customers.

Sample Response

I have always abided by company policies and have never bent the rules. Bending the rules for one customer, will no doubt lead to a downward spiral . Either the customer will expect further rule bending, or other customers will catch on and expect the same treatment. It's just not a wise course of action to take.

Tell me about a time when you failed to communicate effectively?

Evaluation

The ability to communicate well is vital to the role of cabin crew, so you should have plenty of real life examples ready to share. This is your chance to shine, so don't be modest.

Sample Response

Situation:

I remember a trainee apprentice we had in our department who never asked questions and refused all offers of help. Unfortunately, instead of trying to understand her reasons, everyone drew the conclusion that she was a know-it-all and vowed not to offer help in the future.

Action:

Concerned that her progress would suffer, I decided to offer my encouragement and support. It soon became evident from our conversation that she had excessively high expectations of herself and feared looking incompetent. I explained that it was okay to ask questions, and mistakes were expected. I even shared a few of my own early mishaps to lighten the mood.

Result:

Very quickly after that we saw a change in her behaviour. She began asking questions, she was more open to suggestions, and her skills improved immensely.

Reflection:

From this experience, I learnt that things are not always what they appear and we need to be more objective before making rash judgements.

Give an example of when you had to present complex information in a simplified manner in order to explain it to others

Evaluation

As cabin crew, you may be required to break down and convey complex information to customers. For example, if a passenger is afraid of flying, you may need to explain the technicalities of the flight, or if a passenger is hasn't grasped the use of emergency equipment and emergency procedures, you may need to break the information down further.

Your answer here should show that you are able to express knowledge in a clear and simple manner.

Sample Response

Situation:

I remember a client who was interested in having a colour treatment carried out. She was very inquisitive and asked numerous questions, so I could sense that she was concerned about the process and potential damage to her natural hair.

Action:

Not satisfied with a simple nontechnical version, I had to provide a detailed technical breakdown of the whole process. This involved describing the molecular structure of the hair, the effect colour particles have and how they bond to the structure.

Result:

Although I had to occasionally refer to training manuals to emphasise or clarify my point, overall the client was satisfied with my effort. As a direct result, she went ahead with the treatment and was very pleased with the outcome.

Have you ever had to overcome a language barrier?

Evaluation

As cabin crew, you will interact with a variety of people from a broad range of cultures and backgrounds. The ability to relate to others and adapt your communication style is, therefore, very important.

Sample Response

Situation:

During a trip to Africa, I became acquainted with a French lady. She understood my French, the little amount I knew, but she didn't really understand English. Unfortunately, the amount of French I knew wasn't enough to get me through a whole conversation, so I had to improvise.

Action:

I spoke French wherever possible and filled in the gaps with improvised sign language and facial expressions.

Result:

At first it was a little tricky trying to find imaginative ways to communicate, but over time I became much more proficient. I'm sure she was amused by my amateur efforts, but it worked out well and I came away with a new friend.

Reflection:

Now when I encounter this type of communication barrier, I am much more confident in my ability to cope.

Tell me about a time that you had to work as part of a team

Evaluation

The ability to work well within a team is absolutely essential to working as cabin crew. You should, therefore, have plenty of examples that demonstrate this ability.

Sample Response

Situation:

There was a particular time that stands out for me because it was such an unusual occurrence.

It was a usual quiet Tuesday afternoon and only myself, the senior stylist, an apprentice, and the salon manager were on duty. To our surprise, it was as if someone started offering out free chocolate, as clients started to filter through the doors.

Action:

Despite the overwhelming rush, we showed great teamwork as we pulled together and shared our duties.

Even our manager showed great team spirit as she got involved with the hair service.

Result:
As a result of our teamwork, and some free relaxing conditioning treatments, we managed to deliver an outstanding service. Every client went away completely satisfied.

When have you struggled to fit in?

Evaluation

With the constant rotation of crew, there will be some people that you don't immediately hit it off with. The recruiters want to know that you aren't intimidated by such difficulties and are able to move past any struggles.

Sample Response

Situation:
When I started working at Trina's Hair & Beauty, I was joining a very close-knit team who had been together for a number of years.

As a result of the number of trainees they had witnessed come and go over the years, they had become a little reluctant to accept new trainees.

I wouldn't say it was a struggle to fit in as such, but I certainly experienced some growing pains. With remarks such as 'if you are still here then' to contend with, I knew I had to prove myself.

Action:
To show that I was serious about the job, and was not a fly-by-night, I focused a lot of effort on learning my new job. At the same time, I continued to be friendly and respectful of my new colleagues while I made a conscious effort to get to know them.

Result:
As a result of my hard effort, It didn't take long for them to accept me and include me as part of their team. Naturally, I have become closer to some of my colleagues than with others, but we all got on and worked well as a team.

Have you ever experienced difficulties getting along with colleagues?

Evaluation

No matter how hard we try, or how likeable we are, there will always be someone that we don't hit it off with. To say otherwise, would not sound credible.

For the most part, this question is asked to determine your ability to get along with other people and manage adversity. The recruiters want to know that you don't allow conflict to interfere with work.

The best answer should show that you aren't intimidated or confrontational in such situations, but you put in the commitment necessary to build a respectful and healthy working relationship.

Sample Response

Situation:

I remember one co-worker in particular who flat out didn't like me. It didn't matter what I did or said, or whether I tried to avoid or befriend this person.

Action:

After a couple of days of subtle hostility, I decided to assert myself. I diplomatically explained that I acknowledged her dislike for me and I asked for input as to what I must do to create a professional relationship

Result:
Although we never became friends, we were able to maintain more cordial relations thereafter.

Tell us about a challenge you have faced with a colleague

Evaluation

Airlines have a constant rotation of crew on-board each aircraft and, especially within larger airlines, you may not work with the same crew members twice. As a result, it is guaranteed that you will encounter challenging situations with colleagues.

The recruiters want to know that you aren't intimidated by such colleagues or situations, and are prepared to use your initiative to diffuse or mediate as necessary to keep working relationships healthy.

Your answer should demonstrate your willingness to cooperate with others to resolve differences, improve relations, and manage conflicts. It should also display your ability to remain patient and positive in the face of adversity.

Sample Response

Situation:

I do remember one situation where two of my colleagues really didn't hit it off with one another. They were constantly quarrelling and everyone had lost patience with them, but no one wanted to get involved.

Action:

In the end, I decided to take the initiative and act as a sort of mediator to the situation. I was not their manager, so I had to be as tactful as I could so that I wouldn't upset anyone.

I started by explaining that I acknowledged their dislike for each other and then I drew upon the fact that they are both professionals and can, therefore, put aside their differences for the good of the team.

Result:

They had a pretty frank discussion and, although I can't say they ended up the best of friends, they did work out an effective strategy for working more productively together.

Tell me about a disagreement with a colleague

Evaluation

We all have disagreements with colleagues, but they should never get out of control or interfere with work.

You may choose to disclose the details of a conflict situation, but make sure it was minor and didn't interfere with work. Conversely, you may wish to play it safe and declare that while you have had disagreements, they were so minor that you don't really recall the exact details. You could then go on to reiterate some minor examples.

The recruiters want to know that you aren't intimidated by conflicts and have the ability to see things from another person's perspective. Your answer should demonstrate that you are prepared to use your initiative and interpersonal skills to improve relations with colleagues, even in cases where they cannot agree upon certain issues.

Sample Response

Introduction:

Working in a creative environment with other highly skilled professionals, it was natural that we had the occasional clash of ideas. Any disagreements we did have, however, were so relatively minor and insignificant that I would be hard pressed to recall the exact details.

Situation:

Our disagreements were usually as a result of our individual preference towards certain products, styles, magazines or equipment.

Action:

Our debates were never confrontational and they never interfered with our work in any way.

Result:

In fact, some very interesting views emerged from these debates which sometimes resulted in people, including myself, having a slight change in my perspective. So, they were often very educational.

Have you successfully worked with a difficult coworker?

Evaluation

The recruiters want to know that you aren't intimidated by difficult colleagues or situations, and are prepared to use your initiative to deal with the situation as necessary. You will be assessed on how you approached the colleague and how you dealt with the situation.

Your answer should demonstrate your willingness to co-operate with others to resolve differences, improve relations, and manage conflicts. It should also display your ability to remain patient and positive when challenging situations occur.

Sample Response

Situation:

I remember one member of staff was always complaining. Nothing was ever good enough or couldn't possibly work. Everyone had lost patience with her but, because she was so incredibly sensitive, no one said anything.

Action:

I spent some time with her and tactfully told her that it appeared as if she was always putting our ideas down.

Result:

On hearing this feedback she was genuinely horrified at her own behaviour. She explained that she hadn't realised it had made everyone feel that way and agreed that from then on she would try to be more positive.

Very quickly after that we saw a change in her behaviour. She became more conscious of her own attitude and deliberately tried to be more considerate. From that point on, no one could have hoped for a more committed team member.

Have you ever worked with someone you disliked?

Evaluation

There will always be someone that we don't like and to try to convince the recruiter otherwise would not sound honest or credible.

For the most part, this question is asked to determine your ability to get along with other people and manage adversity. The recruiters want to know that you don't allow personal views cause conflict or interfere with work.

The best answer should show that you aren't intimidated or confrontational in such situations, but you put in the commitment necessary to build a respectful and healthy working relationship

Sample Response

Situation:

There was one colleague I worked with that I really found it difficult to get along with personally.

Action:

Instead of focusing on those things I didn't like, I put my personal views aside and focused on the skills she brought to the position.

Result:

My personal view of her never changed, and we never became friends, but we did work productively alongside each other without any problems.

Have you ever acted as a mentor to a coworker?

Evaluation

There may be times when you have to mentor new crew members and the recruiters are trying to assess your ability to lead and mentor your colleagues.

Sample Response

Situation:

I remember when one of our trainees was having problems understanding certain aspects of her course material, and I could see she was becoming increasingly frustrated and self critical.

Action:

Having witnessed her in action, I knew that she was a very bright and talented individual with no obvious lack of skill. So, I determined that her frustrations were probably the result of the pressure she was feeling about her approaching exam.

Concerned at the effect this pressure was having on her, and having experienced the same pressures myself, I decided to offer my support. To reinforce her understanding, I demonstrated some of the techniques she had been struggling with and showed her a few memory tips and tricks which had helped me through my exams.

Result:

My breakdown of the processes, along with the visual demonstration I provided, seemed to make the material much more understandable for her. In the days that followed, she seemed to have a new lease of life and was much more positive. Subsequently, she passed her exams with top grades.

What have you done that shows initiative?

Evaluation

Your answer here should show that you take the initiative when it comes to additional work and demonstrate a natural desire for doing extra tasks willingly.

Sample Response

Situation:

When I began working for my current employer, the inventory system was outdated and the storage room was very messy and disorganised.

Action:

I came in on my day off, cleaned up the mess, organised the store cupboards and catalogued it all on the new inventory forms.

Result:

Thereafter, when orders arrived it was easy to organise and retrieve.

Reflection:

If I'm able to do the task, instead of waiting for the job to be done, I simply do it.

Have you undertaken a course of study, on your own initiative, in order to improve your work performance?

Evaluation

Your answer here should show that you are committed to self-development and take the initiative when it comes to improving yourself and your efficiency.

Sample Response

Situation:

While at Trina's Hair Salon, we were experiencing a spectacular rise in demand for high fashion cuts. I had some creative cutting experience, but nothing that extended to the kind of advanced skill that was required for true high fashion cuts.

Action:

After some consideration, I decided that increasing my creative cutting skills would not only give the salon a competitive advantage, but it would also be a fantastic opportunity for me to move my skills to the next level. So, I took the initiative and, under my own funding, immediately enrolled onto a creative cutting course.

Result:

My new skills proved to be an instant success. Existing clients began recommending me to their friends, which resulted in a massive rise in clientele. Needless to say, my manager was very happy.

Describe an improvement that you personally initiated

Evaluation

The recruiter wants to know that you seek better and more effective ways of carrying out your work and can suggest improvements that will achieve more efficiency.

Your answer here should show that you take the initiative when it comes to improving working methods and standards.

Sample Response

Situation:

While travelling in India, I learnt the art of Indian head massage.

Action:

When I returned to work, I began using my new skill on clients while carrying out the shampoo.

Result:

My massages were becoming such a success, that my manager approached me to request that I train my colleagues. Naturally, I was honoured to oblige.

Describe a new idea or suggestion that you made to your supervisor

Evaluation

The recruiter wants to know that you aren't afraid to take the initiative and suggest improvements.

Sample Response

Situation:

When I was working at Trina's Hair Salon, I had noticed that a lot of our clients wore nail extensions.

Action:

Convinced that the service would be an improvement to our already successful salon, I carried out extensive independent research before presenting the idea to my manager.

Result:

After carrying out her own research, she liked the idea so much that she decided to go ahead with the new service. Within a couple of months, the service was up and running, and we experienced a dramatic increase in new clientele and revenue. I even got a small bonus in my pay packet for my involvement.

Tell me about a problem you encountered and the steps you took to overcome it

Evaluation

The recruiter will be assessing how well you cope with diverse situations, and how you use your judgment and initiative to solve problems.

In answering this question, you need to provide a concrete example of a problem you faced, and then Itemise the steps you took to solve the problem. Your answer should demonstrate a patient and positive attitude towards problem solving.

Sample Response

Situation:

Early in my freelancing career, I experienced several clients who turned up late to their appointments. Some even forgot about their appointments altogether. Rather than just simply being an inconvenience, it was wasting my time and money.

Action:

I considered my options and decided that the best solution would be to send out reminder cards a few days prior to client appointments. For the repeat offenders, I would enforce a late cancellation fee.

Result:

This decision drastically cut the number of late arrivers, and I have never since had a no-show.

Tell me about a problem that didn't work out

Evaluation

No matter how hard we try, there are some instances where a problem just doesn't work out. To say otherwise will not sound honest or credible.

In answering this question, you need to first ensure that the problem was a minor one which had no negative or lasting impact on the company, a colleague or a customer. Try to accentuate the positives and keep your answer specific. Itemise the steps you took to deal with the problem and make it clear that you learnt from the experience.

Sample Response

Situation:

Shortly after I began freelancing, my bank returned a client's cheque to me through lack of funds.

Action:

At first, I was sure it was a mistake caused through an oversight on the part of my client. I made a number of calls, left several messages and even attempted a visit to the clients home, all to no avail.

Several weeks passed and it was clear that I was chasing a lost cause. At this point, I had to decide whether to write off the debt and blacklist the client or visit the Citizens' Advice for advice on retrieving the funds.

Result:

After careful consideration of all the factors involved, I decided to write the debt off as a learning experience.

Reflection:

In hindsight, I realise it was a silly mistake that could easily have been avoided. I have never repeated this error since as I now wait for the funds to clear before carrying out a service.

Have you ever taken the initiative to solve a problem that was above your responsibilities?

Evaluation

Those candidates who demonstrate that they use their initiative and put in extra effort to provide a better and more complete service will surely be looked upon favourably.

Sample Response

Situation:

It had been quite an uneventful afternoon when, all of the sudden, in walked an obviously frantic customer.

From what I could understand, her laptop had contracted a virus while connected to the internet and the system now failed to respond to any commands.

Being a self-employed web designer, the customer was naturally very concerned about the potential loss of data, and earnings.

Unfortunately, while the laptop was still within warranty, it was beyond the companies scope and had to be sent to the manufacturer for restoration. My colleagues, while polite, but could only offer assistance as far as sending the laptop to the manufacturer.

Action:

I could sense the customer was becoming increasingly distressed and, having had previous training in system restoration, I was confident that I could at least safely extract the data from the hard drive.

After talking the customer through the procedure, she granted her permission and I proceeded.

Result:

After some 45 minutes of fiddling with wires and hard drives, the customer's data had been successfully, and safely, extracted. The customer gasped a big sigh of relief as we packaged the laptop off to the manufacturer for repair.

Several weeks later, my line manager received a letter from the customer complimenting my efforts.

Reflection:

I was really pleased that a little effort made such a big difference.

When have you made a bad decision?

Evaluation

We all make decisions that we regret, and to say otherwise will not sound honest or credible.

The recruiter will be assessing whether you have the character to admit and take responsibility for your mistake, whether your decision had a negative impact on customers or the company, and whether you learnt from this mistake?

In answering this question, you need to first ensure that the mistake was a minor one, which had no negative or lasting impact on the company, a colleague or a customer. Try to accentuate the positives and keep your answer specific. Itemise what you did and how you did it. Finally, you need to make it clear that you leant from the mistake and will be certain not to repeat it.

Situation:

Early in my freelance career, I was approached by a salesman who was promoting a protein conditioning system. He described the system as "The newest technology to emerge from years of research. Guaranteed to help heal, strengthen, and protect".

Although I was excited by the concept, I did have my concerns that the system sounded too good to be true. However, the salesman had all the official paperwork to back up his claims, and the literature was thorough and well presented. All these things, combined with the company's full money-back guarantee, made it appear to be a win-win situation, and a risk worth taking. So I invested.

Following my investment, I decided to test the system out on training heads before taking the system public. Unfortunately, several months of using the system passed with no obvious benefits.

Action:

Disappointed with the product, I decided to pursue the full money back guarantee, but the sales number was not recognised, and my letters were returned unopened. Even their website had mysteriously vanished. I soon came to the realisation that I had been taken in by an elaborate scam.

I contacted the Citizens Advice Bureau and Trading Standards, but there was little they could do to retrieve my funds.

Result:

Unfortunately, I never recovered my costs and had to put the mistake down to a learning experience.

Reflection:

Unfortunately, it really was my fault. I should have trusted my gut instinct and carried out thorough research before making my decision. It is a mistake I shall never repeat.

What was the biggest challenge you have faced?

Evaluation

In answering this question, you need to provide a concrete example of a challenge you faced, and then Itemise the steps you took to overcome that challenge.

Your answer should display a patient and positive attitude when challenging situations occur.

Sample Response

Situation:

To be honest, giving up smoking was the biggest challenge. I never thought I could do it, and I had made dozens of attempts that ended in failure.

Action:

Determined not to give in to my withdrawals, I decided I needed an incentive that would pull me through the tough times. Being sponsored for a worthy cause was the perfect solution.

Result:

With a good cause in mind, the following three months were easier than on previous occasions. Not only have I come out the other end a non-smoker, I also managed to raise £2464.00 for Child-line.

Reflection:

Since I gave up smoking, I have gained so much personal insight, and I deal with potentially stressful situations at work so much more effectively now, I feel more energetic, more mentally alert and far calmer now than I ever did before.

Traditional Questions

Cabin Crew

What do you know about the job?

"I know that the service we see as passenger's form only a small portion of what actually goes on in the job. With safety being the primary concern, there are procedures and checks which must be constantly and consistently completed. Then, when things go wrong, cabin crew are there to take control. Moreover, it is a constant process of cleaning and preparation, paperwork and stock checks, tending to passenger comfort and being of service. Clearly the profession is a very demanding one, but it is also a very exciting and fulfilling one for the right person, which I do believe I am."

Do you think the role of cabin crew is glamorous?

"Having thoroughly researched the position, I am aware that the glamour associated with the role is rather superficial. Sure there are benefits of travel, and the crew certainly do make themselves appear glamorous, but the constant travelling between time zones, the long and tiring shifts, unpredictable schedules and irregular working patterns place tough demands on crew and make the job anything but glamorous."

What do you think are the advantages of this position?

"The randomness and variety of the different crew, passenger profiles, roster structure and destinations excite me greatly. They are unique elements that you just don't find in normal nine to five jobs. It's a job I will find rewarding in a number of ways."

What do you think are the disadvantages?

"The obvious disadvantages are the flight delays and cancellations that crew experience. While passengers also experience these issues, crew experience those far more often. This makes for very long and tiring shifts, irregular working patterns and unpredictable schedules.

Moreover, the regular crossing between different time zones can take its toll leading to jet lag and fatigue. Ultimately, though, these challenges are part of the job and, with some advance preparation, they can be managed to a certain degree."

Avoid sounding naive
To deny the obvious drawbacks of the job will only make you sound naive and unprepared. So, be up front about the disadvantages and demonstrate that you have considered these carefully.

What would you change about this position?

"By applying for this position, I have accepted everything that comes with it. I see no point in concerning myself about those things that cannot be changed."

What aspects of customer service are most important to our passengers?

"Passengers want to feel comfortable and looked after by the airline and crew. They want to be assured that crew will listen to and answer their questions, and will be friendly and polite in doing so. If crew are not approachable, passengers feel unwelcome and unsure."

What do you think contributes to passenger frustrations?

"Feeling tired from travelling can cause passengers to feel unusually frustrated. Add to this flight delays, long waiting times and space constrictions, and frustration naturally increases. If the passenger is then greeted by seemingly unwelcoming staff, their tension will certainly rise much further."

Why do you think some passengers vent their frustrations on cabin crew?

"In the first instance, cabin crew wear the airline's uniform. Thus, passengers consider them to be a representative of the airline. Moreover, the passengers spend more time with cabin crew than with any other member of the airline staff, so they simply become an easy target."

What contribution can you make to ensure passengers will fly with us again?

My customer service experience and friendly character style will enable me to deliver a superior standard of service which will make passengers feel welcome, valued and relaxed.

Why should we hire you instead of someone with cabin crew experience?

"Although I might not have cabin crew experience, I have the necessary skills to make an impressive start, and the willingness to learn and improve. Sometimes, employers do better when they hire people who don't have a great deal of repetitive experience. That way, they can train these employees in their methods and ways of doing the job. Training is much easier than un-training."

Why should we hire you for this position rather than another applicant?

"I can't tell you why you should hire me instead of another candidate but, I can tell you why you should hire me."

Are you willing to start as a trainee?

"Yes, absolutely. This is a new area for me, and I believe in getting a good foundation in the basics before progressing. An entry level position will enable me to learn the position inside out, and will give me the opportunity to grow when I prove myself. I also have a great deal of knowledge and work experience, which I'm sure will contribute to my successful progression through training."

How do you feel about the probationary period?

"I can see no problem with a probationary period. I am a fast learner so it shouldn't take me long to prove myself."

How do you feel about working at Christmas, and other special occasions?

"Naturally, I would miss spending time with my friends and family, but my career is important to me and my family and friends respect and appreciate that fact. I am happy to make the sacrifice as necessary."

How do you feel about a formal dress code?

"I have always liked to dress formally and feel very comfortable wearing formal attire. I realise that a standard of dress is necessary in order to project a professional image to the passengers."

This is a long hours culture, is that a problem for you?

"I understand that this a demanding job, but I really do thrive on the challenge of this sort of work and have worked long hours in the past, so I am willing to work whatever hours are necessary to get the work done."

This position will involve relocating, how will you adjust to the different lifestyle?

"I realise that this position involves transfers, and I bore that in mind when I applied. I am fully aware of what to expect from the research I have done and would welcome the different lifestyle."

How do you feel about the routine tasks and irregular hours of this job?

"I accept that every role carries with it a certain amount of routine in order to get the job done. If my job involves repetitive work, it is my responsibility to carry it out to the best of my abilities. As for irregular hours I would expect to have an indication of my core hours, but will work the hours that are necessary in order to fulfil the requirements of the role."

Do you feel confident in your ability to handle this position?

"Yes, absolutely. I'm very confident in my abilities. I'm familiar with the basic job requirements and I learn quickly. It undoubtedly will take time and effort on my part, but I'm more than willing to devote that time and effort."

Do you feel ready for a more responsible position?
"Absolutely. I believe that eight years experience working closely with customers, has prepared me professionally and personally to move up to this role. My customer care and teamwork skills have been finely tuned over the years, and I know I am capable of greater achievements."

How will you cope with the change in environment?
"I welcome the challenge of learning about and adapting to a new environment, that's one of the reasons I'm seeking to make a career change right now. Any major change, while always containing some challenge is a chance to grow, learn, and advance."

The Airline
Have you ever flown with us?
"Yes, I have had the fortunate opportunity to fly with Fly High Airlines on several occasions now. With the attentive crew, outstanding meal service and comfortable seating, I

always feel as though I am flying first class. I am now a frequent flyer and very happy customer. I now hope to join your team in providing this fantastic service."

How would you rate us against our competitors?
Example 1
"It's so difficult to be objective, and I really don't like to slight your competition."

Example 2
"My experiences with each of the airlines I have flown with have all been good, and I never had a problem or cause for complaint. An advantage of Fly High Airlines, however, is the attentiveness of the crew. They really take care of all their passengers and do everything to make the flight as pleasant as possible. I have always been made to feel welcome on board your flights."

Do you think we have a good reputation?
"Absolutely! Through my own experience, I have encountered attentive and efficient crew, fantastic meals and comfortable seating. In researching the airline, it appears that others agree with these observations.

The variety of awards the airline has received over the years is a sure testament to its fantastic reputation."

What is the worst thing you have heard about us?

"The worst thing I have heard about Fly High Airlines is that competition for jobs is fierce because it is such a terrific airline. Everything else I have heard, have been overly positive."

Is there anything you think we do badly?

"In conducting my research into the airline, I haven't come across anything to suggest that you are doing anything badly. In fact, I have discovered quite the opposite.

Plus, I am sure you wouldn't enjoy your current success and be receiving so many awards for excellence if you were doing anything really wrong."

How do you feel about working for a small airline?

"I have always valued the feeling of a small company. They haven't become large and impersonal and I like the potential for being involved in the growth of the airline."

How do you feel about working for a large airline?

"I welcome the opportunity to work in a large, developed and well known airline such as this. The resources and potential for advancement are not available in smaller airlines. I'd be proud to apply my skills and abilities to the excellence that flourishes here."

Have you applied to any other airlines?
"Although it is taking a bit of a risk, I haven't applied to other airlines because I am set on working for you. I wanted to see how my application went with you before I considered other options."

If another airline offered you a job, would you take it?
"Because I am set on making cabin crew my future career, if I did not get this job with you, then I would have to consider other airlines. However, Fly High Airlines are at the very top of my list and I would be naturally disappointed not to get the job with you."

Career History
Why did you leave your last job?
No opportunities
"While I enjoyed working for my previous employer, and appreciate the skills I developed while I was there, I felt I was not being challenged enough in the job. After working

my way up through the company, there were no further opportunities for advancement."

Redundancy
"I survived the first layoffs, but unfortunately this one got me."

Temporary position
"The job was only a temporary position which I took to broaden my experience."

Why have you had so many jobs?
Broaden experience
"I wanted to experience different jobs to broaden my knowledge, skills and experience. This has provided me with a very valuable and rounded skill set."

Temporary positions
"Due to the lack of full time opportunities in my area, I was only able to secure short term contracts."

Youth
In my youth, I was unsure about the direction I wanted to take in my career. I have matured a great deal since those

days and am now interested in establishing myself into a long term opportunity.

Why were you fired?

The recruiters will not care if a termination was unjust, unfair or has a good explanation, a termination is a big red flag and will mark the end of your interview so you need to do everything you can to avoid disclosing it.

If you do decide that honesty is the best policy for you, then here are some tips to help you lighten the blow.

Incompatibility

"I was desperate for work and took the job without fully understanding the expectations. It turned out that my competencies were not a right match for the employer's needs so we agreed that it was time for me to move on to a position that would be more suitable. I certainly learnt a great deal from this experience, and it's not a mistake I will ever repeat."

Personal reasons

"I had been going through a rough patch in my personal life which, unfortunately, upset my work life. It is regrettable and my circumstances have now changed, but I really wasn't in the position to avoid it at the time"

Never:

- Badmouth previous employers, colleagues or bosses.
- Place blame
- Tell lies
- Reveal team incompatibility

Why were you unemployed for so long?

Study

"I wanted to broaden my knowledge base, so I went back into full time study."

Travel

"I wanted to experience the world before settling into a long term career. I am now well travelled and ready to commit."

Youth

"In my youth, I felt confused about the direction I wanted my career to take. I am now much more mature and certain in my desired direction."

Personal reasons

"Personal circumstances prohibited me from taking gainful employment, however, circumstances have now changed and I am ready to get back to work."

It is better to say that you chose to take time off between jobs than it is to give the impression that you were unemployable.

Why did you stay with the same employer for so long?

"I was there for several years, but in a variety of different roles. The opportunities for growth were fantastic so it felt as though I was undergoing frequent changes without actually changing employer. I didn't see the need to move on."

Why have you decided to change professions at this stage of your career?

"This career turnaround hasn't come suddenly. I have always wanted to become cabin crew and have been gradually mastering the skills needed to perform its tasks. I have now reached a point in my life where I am prepared to make the career and lifestyle change. I want to take advantage of that opportunity while it is presented to me."

What do you like about your current job?

"Rather than pick out the little details of the routine work, here are three general things. First is customer satisfaction. Seeing a client's face glow with happiness when their hair is transformed gives me an intense feeling of pride. Second is the interaction I get with my colleagues and clients. Finally, I enjoy being creative and finding new ways to please the customer."

Which particular aspect of your work do you find most frustrating?

"That's an interesting question because I am, generally speaking, a tolerant person. Slow periods can be sources of frustration, but at times like that I put more effort into advertising and establishing new clientele. That way, the slow periods don't last long."

Character Traits

Are you an introvert or extrovert?

"Actually, I would describe myself as an ambivert because I enjoy social interaction, but am equally happy to spend time alone in my own company."

What makes you stand out from the crowd?

"My friendly and positive nature certainly defines me as a person and makes me stand out from the crowd. I adopt a very optimistic view in every aspect of my life and refuse to allow external circumstances to negatively affect my state."

If you had to characterise yourself in one sentence, what would you say?

"I am a friendly and approachable person, who is sincere and very optimistic about life."

Rate yourself on a scale from 1 to 10

"I would rate myself as an 8. I always give my best, but in doing so I increase my skills. I, therefore, always see room for improvement."

How would a friend describe you?

"My friends would describe me as sociable, cheerful and optimistic. They would also say I am someone who thinks fast on my feet and stays calm in adverse situations."

How would an enemy describe your character?

"I suppose they might say that I am tenacious because I don't give in without a struggle, but am realistic about my limits. They might say I am brave because I am prepared to confront issues when there is a need, but I weigh the consequences and don't act irresponsibly. And, maybe, driven because I push for what I want, but can back off when advisable to do so."

How have you changed in the last five years?
"I feel like I have matured rather than aged five years. The skills I have acquired and the qualities I have developed have changed me enormously, and I know there are parts of me that are still not being utilised half as effectively as they could be. My customer care and communication skills have definitely been improved, and I have a better ability to use my initiative and think on my feet."

Background

These kinds of questions draw from personal experience, and are fairly easy to answer, so they are often used to settle candidates into an interview. Selectors also use background questions as a reference point from which to introduce the more role-specific questions.

Recruiters are likely to probe with follow up questions if they think there are revealing aspects about qualities they wish to explore (or potential problems, such as long/ frequent periods of sickness).

Tip: Be positive about the work you do, and about your outside interests. Negative or pessimistic attitudes are unlikely to advance your cause! Also, if you consider the kind of qualities selectors are trying to identify, you will be better able to phrase your replies to make the most favourable impression.

Customer Focus

How would you define good customer service?

"Good customer service is about constantly and consistently meeting customer's expectations by providing a friendly, efficient and reliable service throughout the life of the service and/or product.

Excellent customer service is about exceeding customer's expectations by going beyond the call of duty. I believe that because no two customers are the same, they deserve to receive a service that is tailored to their individual needs. This is where a service moves beyond being just a satisfactory one, and becomes an excellent one."

What do you think constitutes poor customer service?

"Poor service is when customers are treated with disrespect and provided with a poor quality product and/ or service by rude, ignorant and unhelpful staff."

Do you think the customer is always right?

"Whilst every customer is important, they are certainly not always right. Those who exhibit abusive behaviour, or do anything to compromise safety are straying beyond the boundary."

When have you witnessed good customer service?

"I remember when I visited a local restaurant for a luncheon. It had just turned 3pm on a Wednesday afternoon and, much to mine and the management's surprise, they were exceptionally busy with only three waiting staff on duty. Despite the overwhelming rush our waitress, Claire, was very polite and helpful. The staff showed great teamwork as they managed to pull together and deliver an outstanding service."

When have you witnessed poor customer service?

"I needed a particular material for a dress I was making. In most stores the salesperson would give me a quick 'no' before I finished explaining what I was looking for. I hadn't really noticed until I experienced the opposite service in another smaller fabric store."

What do you enjoy about providing customer care?

"The most enjoyable aspect I would have to say is that because I genuinely care about my client's satisfaction, it rewards me personally when I know that they are happy with the job I did. This, in turn, drives me to do better."

What do you dislike about providing customer care?

"Providing good customer care can be a challenge, and some people may view that negatively, but I view each challenge as an opportunity to develop and grow. So, because I am committed to developing myself, I welcome and enjoy the challenges of providing customer care. It is something I have become very good at."

What do you find most challenging about providing customer service?

"Providing customer service is a challenge in itself. Because people are unpredictable by their very nature, you have to always expect the unexpected and be prepared to go beyond the call of duty and deal with issues as they arrive."

Team Spirit

How would you define teamwork?

"Teamwork is a group of people who work cooperatively together to achieve a common goal. They make a coordinated effort and each individual contributes their unique skills and ideas to the task."

Do you prefer to work alone or as part of a team?

"I am happy either way, and equally efficient at both. So, whether I prefer to work alone or in a team would depend on the best way to complete the job.

I do, however, have a preference towards team spirit. As well as the interaction, there is greater satisfaction when you share the joy of completing a task."

Are you a team player?

"Absolutely I am. As you will have observed during the group assessments, I interact well with others, and readily adapt to new people. I am a good listener, I respect other people's opinions and I can be relied on to contribute to the overall goal.

In fact, my previous supervisor used to say that my infectious optimism created excitement in other team members and resulted in a greater team effort and higher output."

What role do you assume in a team situation?

"I am whatever I need to be. If a situation comes up and someone needs to take charge, then I will. But if someone else has already taken charge and is solving it, I will follow their lead."

What do you enjoy about working as part of a team?

"There's nothing like being part of a great team where you can learn from the other members, bounce ideas off one another, and share achievements and rewards. There is a unique feeling of camaraderie that can never be experienced from working alone."

What do you least enjoy about working as part of a team?

"People not pulling their weight can be frustrating. However, I've noticed that such people simply lack enthusiasm or confidence, and that energetic and cheerful coworkers can often change that."

What do you find most challenging about being part of a team?

"The most challenging aspect is inspiring and motivating other team members. Each has different needs and is motivated by different things."

Are you happy to be supervised by people who are younger than yourself?

"Absolutely. I don't consider age to be an important factor. What matters is a person's credibility, professionalism and competency."

Communication

What is the importance of having good communication skills?

"The ability to speak clearly, listen actively and comprehend effectively is vital for our successful interaction with others, and continued growth."

How confident are you about addressing a group?

"I used to be nervous about speaking in front of a group, yet I found that preparation, practice and knowing my subject helped me overcome this, I now have no problem addressing a group."

Rate your communication skills on a scale of 1 to 10.

"I would rate myself as an 8. I always give my best, but in doing so I increase my skills. I, therefore, always see room for improvement."

Do you think your lack of language skills will affect your ability to perform the job?

"I admit my language skills are a little light, however, I am working on increasing my language fluency and, should I be offered the position, I will be sure to work on increasing my language abilities even further."

Hypothetical

Hypothetical questions present candidates with difficult real-life situations, where almost any answer can be challenged.

A good way to approach these questions is to consider the feelings of everyone involved, and think about the implications for your colleagues and the airline.

Prove to the recruiters that you would be proactive and do your best to resolve the situation using your own initiative, whilst remembering that you could ask for the help of the more experienced crew if necessary.

If you have followed these guidelines and are still challenged, the recruiter may be testing your ability to manage conflict or stress. Bear in mind that if you are not cabin crew yet, you cannot really be expected to know the best reply so do not be tricked into entering into an argument with the recruiter.

In either case it is important to remain calm and focused, and to demonstrate that, although you appreciate there are many aspects to each situation, you would always be trying to find acceptable solutions.

If you really can't think of a solution, you can simply say, "That is a new area for me so I am afraid I can't really answer that, but I enjoy acquiring new knowledge and I do learn quickly."

You are in flight at 30,000 feet. How would you handle a passenger if he became irate about his lost baggage?
"At 30,000 feet, there is not a lot you can do about the baggage, so the problem at hand is reassuring the passenger and avoiding further disruption.

First, I would try to manoeuvre the passenger somewhere more private where they can explain the situation. I would then apologise for the mishandling, and offer to assist on the ground by escorting him to the proper people who can help."

What would you do if the seat belt signs are on due to turbulence, but a passenger gets up to go to the toilet?

"Because of the importance of passenger safety, I would advise the passenger to wait until the seat belt signs have been turned off. If the passenger really cannot wait, I will follow the corporate policy for dealing with such a situation."

How would you handle a passenger who is intoxicated?

"I would not provide any more alcoholic beverages. I would encourage food, and offer a cup of tea or coffee. If the situation worsens beyond my control, I would inform my senior and seek assistance from the other crew members."

What would you do if a commercially important passenger complained about a crying child?

"I would apologise to the passenger and offer my assistance to the guardian of the child."

How would you deal with a passenger who is scared of flying?

"Being aware of what to expect, and just realising that a plane's wings are supposed to flex and move around gently in flight, can help relieve anxiety. Similarly, the collection of bumps and bangs that always accompany a flight can be made less fearsome if they are expected. So, I would try to comfort the passenger by talking them through the flight, and reassuring them of any strange noises they may hear.

I would advise them where I can be found, and show them the call bell. I would then check on them periodically throughout the flight."

How would you deal with a passenger who is not, right but believes he is right?

"I would explain the company's rules and policies to the passenger in a calm, professional and positive manner. Hopefully, this should clarify any misconceptions that the passenger may have."

How would you handle a colleague who is being rude or racist?

"I would act immediately to put a stop to any racist or rude behaviour by making it clear to the person that their behaviour is not acceptable. If he or she continues, I would then report it to proper authority."

If you spotted a colleague doing something unethical or illegal, what would you do?

"I would act immediately to put a stop to any unethical or illegal activity. I would try to document the details of the incident and try to collect any physical evidence. Then I would report it to my senior."

What would you do if you suspect that a passenger is suspicious or a high risk to passengers?

"I would keep watch before reporting to the senior any abnormal behaviour indicating a suspicious passenger."

What would you do and how would you react in a hijacking?

"I would remain calm, and follow the emergency guidelines and procedures."

How would you act in an emergency such as a crash landing?

"As soon as I get the warning that something is going to happen, I would get a plan together in my mind. I would stay calm and in control and follow the emergency guidelines and procedures."

What three items would you choose to have if trapped on a desert island?

"The three items I would have to have would be a medical kit containing various items such as medicines, water purification tablets, surgical blades, plasters and cotton wool. Second, I would have my survival kit containing essential items such as a compass, a striker and flint, torch, waterproof matches, a magnifying glass, and fish hooks and line. Third, a good survival guidebook."

If you were trapped on a desert island, what book would you want?

With this question, you could respond with a serious answer, such as:

"I would have to have an SAS survival guide."

Or, you can opt for personality, such as:

"I would want Robert Frost's Collection of Poems, because it would keep me occupied and in positive spirits while I wait for rescue."

If you were going to Mars, what three items would you take?

"First, I would take a trained astronaut. Second, sufficient food for the journey and finally, enough fuel for the return trip."

Adversity

Have you stretched the truth today to gain a favourable outcome?

"Absolutely not. I haven't tried to be someone I am not, because I wouldn't want to get the job that way. To do so would be such a short term gain because eventually I would be found out."

How would you respond if we told you that you have been unsuccessful on this occasion?

"Naturally, I will be a disappointed if I do not secure this job with you because it is something I really want, I feel ready for it, and I have had plenty to contribute. However, I am not one to give up quickly. I will think about where I went wrong and how I could have done better, and I would then take steps towards strengthening my candidacy."

What would you say if I said your skills and experience were below the requirements of this job?

"I would ask what particular aspects of my skills and experience you felt were lacking and address each one of those areas with examples of where my skills and experiences do match your requirements. I would expect that after this discussion you would be left in no doubt about my ability to do this job."

Aren't you overqualified for this position?

"I wouldn't say that I am overqualified, but certainly fully qualified. With more than the minimal experience, I offer immediate returns on your investment. Don't you want a winner with the skill sets and attitudes to do just that?"

What question could I ask that would intimidate you?

"I can't think of any question that would intimidate me. This is probably the most intimidating question."

How would you rate me as a recruiter?

"First, I'd give you high marks for your people skills. You helped me feel at ease right away, which made it easier for me to answer the questions. I'd also rate you highly on the creativity of the questions, and their thoroughness. By probing me as carefully as you have, you've given me a better opportunity to secure this position. You've given me a complete picture of what to expect at Fly High Airlines, and it confirms my belief that this is where I want to work."

I'm not sure you are suitable for the position. Convince me.

"I am absolutely suitable. In fact, I am confident that I am perfect for this position.

You are looking for someone who is customer focused. Well, as you can see from my résumé, I have worked in client facing roles for eight years so have had plenty of experience dealing with the various aspects. I also run a successful business that relies on customer satisfaction. The fact that I am still in business, and have a solid and increasing client base, is a clear testament to my abilities.

Furthermore, you need someone who has a calm approach, and retains their composure in the face of adversity. Again, I have demonstrated this capability on several occasions throughout my career.

Beyond this, I have a friendly and optimistic character. I am hard working, I thrive on challenges and will always strive to deliver the highest standard of service to your passengers.

I am confident that my skills, experience and personal qualities will complement your existing team and allow me to make a positive contribution to the airline's ongoing success."

Do you work well under pressure?

"Absolutely. Because pressure is the result of a new challenge, I perceive pressure as an opportunity to develop and grow. The more challenges I experience, the better my skills become, and the less I feel the pressure of subsequent challenges. So, because I am committed to developing myself, I welcome the challenges of pressure."

How would I know you were under pressure?

"I disguise my pressure well, therefore, I would hope that it wouldn't be obvious enough to notice."

What types of people annoy you or try your patience?

"That's an interesting question, because I am a very tolerant person. However, there are instances where my patience is put to the test, but I am able to control myself and my emotions, so I never let my patience move beyond the testing stage."

Do you have difficulties tolerating people with different views than you?

"No. I recognise that everyone has their own views, and that they may not always correspond with my own. Differing views and personalities are what make us individual, so I don't let other people's views or interests affect how I feel about them."

How often do you lose your temper?

"I never lose my temper. I regard that sort of behaviour as counterproductive and inappropriate. By losing your temper, you cannot possibly resolve a problem. Even if you're completely right, losing your temper often destroys your ability to convince others of this."

What makes you angry or impatient?

"Anger to me means loss of control, and I'm not the kind of person who loses control. It is counterproductive and inappropriate, and doesn't gain anything of value.

When I feel stress building up, instead of getting angry or impatient, I take a deep breath and begin to focus on the positives. The results are quite dramatic, my whole demeanour changes very rapidly,"

How do you handle criticism?

"As long as the criticism is fair and constructive, I listen to it and remain gracious. I thank them for their candid feedback, express regret over the situation and modify my future behaviour accordingly."

Closing

So you do still wish us to consider you for this position?

"Absolutely! Having had this chance to meet you and learn more about the airline and position, I am even more eager than before. I am convinced that this is the opportunity I am seeking, and I know I can make a positive contribution."

Would you take this job if we offered it to you?

"Yes, definitely. I was eager as soon as I saw the job opening on your web site. More than that though, actually meeting potential colleagues and finding out more about the airline and the position has clarified still further what an exciting challenge it would be to work here."

When are you available to start if offered the position?

"I have the energy and enthusiasm to start straight away. All I need is a week's notice and I'm ready."

Where do you picture yourself in five years?

"I very much hope that I shall be with Fly High Airlines in five years time. By which time, I will have made a significant contribution to the airline, will have become an experienced senior member of the cabin crew team, and will be working on new ways to advance my career further."

If offered the job, how long will you stay with us?

"I'm approaching this job with a long term view. I hope to make enough of a contribution the airline, that I can move up through the ranks to become an experienced senior member of the cabin crew team."

Do you have any reservations about working here?

"I don't have any reservations at this point. I see this position as a fine opportunity, and the airline as one I would be proud to be an employee of."

Can we contact previous employers for references?

"Yes, absolutely. I'm confident that all my references will be favourable and will confirm what we've discussed here today."

Ask the right questions

This section of the interview is a real chance for you to shine and set yourself apart from all the other candidates. Therefore, it is a good idea to prepare one or two intelligent questions in advance.

The questions you ask, and how you ask them, say a lot about you, your motives, your depth of knowledge about the airline and the position itself.

Guidelines

The questions you ask should follow these guidelines:

Don't ask questions that could be easily answered through your own research.

Ask questions which demonstrate a genuine interest in and knowledge of the airline and the position.

Demonstrate that you know just that little bit more than is required.

Question About Suitability

Asking recruiters to raise their concerns about your suitability will provide you with an opportunity to follow up and reassure the recruiter.

Do you have any reservations about my ability to do this job?

What do you foresee as possible obstacles or problems I might have?

Is there anything else I need to do to maximise my chances of getting this job?

How does my background compare with others you have interviewed?

Is there anything else you'd like to know?

What do you think are my strongest assets and possible weaknesses?

Do you have any concerns that I need to clear up in order to be a considered candidate?

Questions About the Recruiter

Asking recruiters about their views and experience in the job or working with the airline will demonstrate your genuine interest and motives.

How did you find the transition in relocating to ...?

Why did you choose to work at ... airlines?

What is it about this airline that keeps you working here?

It sounds as if you really enjoy working here, what have you enjoyed most about working for ... airlines?

General Questions

How would you describe the company culture?

I feel my background and experience are a good fit for this position, and I am very interested. What is the next step?

Yes, when do I start?

No Questions

I did have plenty of questions, but we've covered them all during our discussions. I was particularly interested in ... but we've dealt with that thoroughly.

I had many questions, but you've answered them all you have been so helpful. I'm even more excited about this opportunity than when I applied.

Questions to Avoid

You should avoid asking questions such as those following as they will make you appear selfishly motivated.

How many day's holiday allowances will I receive?

What is the salary?

When will I receive a pay increase?

How many free flights will my family receive?

Can I request flights to ...?

What Next?

You've made it through the entire interview process, you've navigated your way through the group interview and woo'd the interviewers with your answers during the final interview, and now comes the hardest part of all. Waiting for the golden call.

I kid you not, this is tough and weeks will feel like years as you await to discover your fate.

Hopefully this final step will help to get you through it, although I'm not sure anything can help beyond getting the phone to ring. But here goes, let's do this.

JOURNAL THE EXPERIENCE

During this step five, all I want you to do is take some time to write a short journal of what happened during your recruitment experience.

Journaling will achieve two very important things:

1. Get it out of your system
Whatever has happened, you're not going to stop thinking and analysing it to death, so you might as well go full

steam ahead and write it all out. Get it out of your head and onto paper so that you can at least start to make some sense out of everything. It may even help you feel more relaxed.

2. Give you a reference point for the future

The second and, most important, reason for journaling is that there is a chance that the conditions weren't right for you on this particular occasion and it will help you immensely if you keep a log of your experience to help you prepare for the next opportunity.

As time goes on, you begin to forget what you could have improved upon or what you learnt, so journalling soon after the interview is over while they are fresh in your mind will lead you towards being successful later on. Remember to be as objective as possible for best results.

Follow up

Following the final interview, airlines aim to follow up with candidates within two to eight weeks. This is the time that is most difficult, and it is unlikely that you will sleep soundly as you wait of the outcome of the interview.

If you are successful, you can expect to receive a job offer from the recruitment department by email, telephone and / or letter within the noted time frame. ,

For those candidates who have been successful, you will be advised of the various pre joining clearance requirements. These may include:

- Preemployment medical test
- Reference checks
- Joining forms

Once the required steps of the process have been completed, the airline will make the necessary arrangements to deliver the employment contract and relevant documentation. You will also be given final clearance to resign from your current employer.

Coping with setbacks

It may seem counter intuitive to provide coping strategies for rejection in an interview guidance book, however, in an industry such as this, where supply exceeds demand, rejection is an unfortunate outcome that some candidates will ultimately face.

So, rather than be crushed by this outcome, I have put

together the following tips for coping with, learning from and moving forward following a setback.

Prepare

The popular saying 'Prepare for the worst, but hope for the best' certainly applies in interview scenarios. If you attend the interview with an open mind, your attitude will be more relaxed, you will be better prepared and your coping abilities will be greatly enhanced.

Assess

Faced with rejection, it can be easy to misplace blame on yourself, others or on the general circumstances. But, if you are to learn and grow from your experience, you must be objective and logical in your assessment, rather than making rash and unsubstantiated assumptions.

Firstly, you need to reflect on your own performance to establish any possible areas for improvement. You can then make adjustments as necessary and shift your focus to the next opportunity.

Firstly, you need to reflect on your own performance to establish any possible areas for improvement. In this assessment, you could ask:

- Did I dress appropriately?

- How did I sound?

- Did I arrive on time?

- Did I remember to smile?

- Did I appear confident and relaxed?

- Could my answers have been improved?

- Did I maintain appropriate eye contact?

- Did I establish rapport with the recruiter?

If this assessment identifies any weaknesses, you can make adjustments as necessary and shift your focus to the next opportunity.

Accept

Sometimes factors exist that are beyond your control and the unfortunate outcome may not have been directly influenced by your performance at all. In this instance, all you can do is accept the outcome and shift your focus to the next opportunity.

Be positive

Whatever the reason for rejection, it is important to treat each setback as a learning experience. So, don't become obsessive or overly critical, keep an open mind and be open to change if necessary. By handling the setback in this way, you will move forward and succeed much more quickly.